COMMAND AT ANTIETAM

Lincoln, McClellan and Lee

DAVID L. KELLER

THE
History
PRESS

Published by The History Press
Charleston, SC
www.historypress.com

Cover images: Images of McLellan, Lincoln and Lee courtesy of the Library of Congress. Image of Lincoln visiting the Antietam battlefield courtesy of the Library of Congress.

First published 2021

Manufactured in the United States

ISBN 9781467146739

Library of Congress Control Number: 2021931143

Notice: The information in this book is true and complete to the best of our knowledge. It is offered without guarantee on the part of the author or The History Press. The author and The History Press disclaim all liability in connection with the use of this book.

Dedicated to…

*The U.S. National Park and U.S. National Battlefields
professional staff and volunteers.*

They keep history alive.

CONTENTS

Acknowledgements

S pecial thanks to all the outstanding writers who have contributed to the history of Antietam/Sharpsburg. Their work has inspired me to add to the body of knowledge. Civil War buffs around Sharpsburg have been a great help in sharing their knowledge with me and providing comments on my early drafts. Several Antietam Battlefield guides, who prefer to be anonymous, provided comments and input on this project that were invaluable. While we may not always agree on conclusions, we appreciate our enthusiasm for Civil War history. Very special thanks to historian and UPS park ranger Matt Borders for his guidance through the details of Antietam. Also, thanks to my friends Warren Johnson from Hagerstown, Maryland; Jane Vanderhook of Shepherdstown, West Virginia; Dr. Jon Willen of the Washington, D.C. Civil War Round Table; and Mike Movis from the Civil War Round Table Congress for helping me connect with these new friends.

Three other special friends have consistently encouraged me throughout this process: Dan Joyce and Doug Dammann of the Kenosha Civil War Museum and Waite Rawls of the American Civil War Museum have always been there for me. The board of directors of the Camp Douglas Restoration Foundation took up the slack while I spent hours on this project.

All the maps in this book are provided by Bradley M. Gottfried, whose book *The Maps of Antietam* was a valuable tool on the battle. Special thanks to Brad for creating the first map, *Peninsula Campaign, April–May 1862*, for this book.

Sarah Richards Burton deserves special thanks for proofreading and editing my drafts. Kate Jenkins, acquisition editor at The History Press, was of great encouragement and provided valuable guidance in the early process of publication. Ryan Finn, senior editor, also provided effective and understanding assistance in the publication of this book. Natasha Walsh provided the design of the cover.

Finally, thanks to my understanding wife, Linda. While we share office space in our home, my books, papers, magazines and maps have taken way more share of the space than I deserve.

INTRODUCTION

RESEARCH

Conducting research on the Civil War offers unique challenges. Published material from historians varies greatly. Early publications supporting the "Lost Cause" reflect a Southern bias that is more emotional than factual. Later works range from personal opinions to well-researched investigative reporting. All reach conclusions based on analysis of the same data, and these conclusions may vary greatly.

Most of the firsthand information on the war comes from a series of sources. Diaries, letters and journals are an excellent source of first-person observations. Diaries are the most significant; however, these documents represent one person's recollection of the war at the time of each entry. Letters are written for the benefit of the receiver. A description of action written to a mother is significantly different than the description of the same event sent to a close pal. Journals offer long, detailed descriptions of war events. Many of these were written well after the war and contain the fragilities of and selective memory. In addition, some were written to justify military pensions, political ambition or wartime behavior and are therefore self-serving. Similarly, autobiographies and biographies written by friends or close associates are often written to justify war activities and preserve the good name of the subject.

Newspaper accounts of the day often contain excellent information. However, newspapers also reflect regional and political bias and often contain factual errors.

Official records contain written material by individuals with understandable biases. Campaign reports written after the event may include material to support the writer's actions or to counter criticism received. Orders and direct communications during actions reflect the pressures of the moment and frequently contain understandable errors. It is nearly impossible to understand individual mindsets or motivations at the times these documents were produced. For example, General George McClellan was accused of writing "extravagant reports" that "exculpated his failed campaigns."[1]

When drawing conclusions from material available, the researcher is challenged to use a preponderance of information rather than reaching conclusions on anecdotal information or biased views.

Frequently, historians have assessed General George B. McClellan based on psychological and personality issues during his career. For an excellent summary of these issues, see Thomas Rowland's book, *George B. McClellan and Civil War History*.[2] Rather than dwell on these issues, I have chosen to evaluate only his military actions and the results of these actions. The use of personality traits has also colored the actions of Robert E. Lee and Abraham Lincoln. Again, I have chosen to avoid these issues.

Traditional critics of General McClellan are often considered Unionist historians. While I am critical of McClellan's actions, I do not consider myself a Unionist. Rather, I have attempted to evaluate his performance while acknowledging the important positions taken by his supporters.

THE WAR

From the first shots at Fort Sumter to the Siege of Petersburg, the Confederacy could not win the Civil War. Obviously, no one could predict the outcome. Both President Lincoln and President Davis initially believed that the conflict could be ended in a short period of time. Events proved them both wrong. The ultimate separation of the Confederacy from the Union could be achieved only by decisions made in the North.

The Confederacy lacked the men and resources to effectively carry the war to the North. Table 1 shows the disparity of critical resources. Only in cotton, rice, beef cattle and swine did the South outproduce the North.

Table 1

Item	North	South
Population (non-slave)	18.5 million	5.5 million
Railroad Mileage	20,000 miles	9,000 miles
Manufacturing: Number of factories	100,500	20,600
Manufacturing: Value of products	$1,500 million	$155 million
Bank Deposits	$189 million	$47 million

Source: The Civil War, *Bruce Catton*

The Confederacy's capacity to arm and equip an army was significantly limited by resources. As the war continued, the South's ability to provide for the needs of its soldiers and civilians was made most difficult by the limited resources available. Additionally, an effective Union blockade led to a shortage of resources and needed supplies for the Confederacy, such as medicine, that were already in short supply or not readily available in the South.

Without substantial outside support, the South was destined to lose a traditional war. The only hope for the South was a short war with early military victories to convince the mixed feelings in the political parties of the North that allowing secession was acceptable. Assistance from foreign powers, including economic assistance and blockade running, was not enough to offset the economic advantages of the North. Assistance from Europe, specifically England and France, provided meaningful material support to the Confederacy; however, this support was limited by political considerations and was insufficient to meet the minimum needs of the South. Canada, while providing a haven for Confederate spies and escaped prisoners, was of little value to the Confederacy.

Success of the separation of the Confederate states from the Union was dependent on the North permitting the separation. This permission was not likely to be obtained through traditional military means. Rather, actions by the South that would result in the North tiring of the conflict were the only satisfactory alternative for the Confederacy. These actions needed to prolong the conflict through less expensive nonconventional military operations to the point where tiring of the conflict would change the political position of the North. Obtaining stronger support from England and France, including the possibility of official government recognition of the Confederate state, might change the position of the Union. This concept of the weak versus the strong has modern examples. The actions in North Vietnam and from the Vietcong in Vietnam represent a graphic example of war fatigue by a stronger opponent, the United States. Current conditions in the Middle East offer present-day illustrations of this phenomenon at work.

The Battle of Antietam was fought on September 17, 1862, seventeen months after the surrender of Fort Sumter on April 14, 1861, and more than two and a half years before the surrender of General Lee at Appomattox on April 9, 1865. Circumstances surrounding the Battle of Antietam represent specific factors that were pivotal in determining the results of the Civil War. Analyzing the actions and results of those actions of the primary players—President Abraham Lincoln, George B. McClellan and Robert E. Lee—offers a projection of the future of the war.

This book reviews the time leading up to the battle at Antietam, the battle itself and the results of the decisions and actions of the commands of Lincoln, McClellan and Lee.

The Union description of the Battle of Antietam is used throughout the text, understanding that the Confederacy referred to the battle as the Battle of Sharpsburg. The spelling of Harper's Ferry from the period is used, rather than the current spelling, Harpers Ferry. Troop numbers during the Maryland Campaign are a source of disagreement. I have used either confirmed information or numbers that are generally accepted. *Numbers and Losses at Battle of Antietam*, NPS Handout, ANB, identified troop strengths and served as a valuable source.

List of Maps

Timeline of Events

April 1862	McClellan departs Washington, D.C., to begin the Peninsula Campaign.
August 3, 1862	Peninsula Campaign is over. McClellan begins moving troops north.
August 29–30, 1862	Second Battle of Bull Run (Manassas) takes place.
September 2, 1862	President Abraham Lincoln removes Major General John Pope from command after the Second Battle of Bull Run (Manassas), appointing Major General George B. McClellan in command of all units in the vicinity of Washington, D.C.
September 4, 1862	Confederate General Robert E. Lee invades Maryland.
September 7, 1862	General McClellan begins pursuit of Lee, moving his headquarters to the field.
September 14, 1862	Battle of South Mountain and Investment of Harper's Ferry take place.

September 17, 1862	Battle of Antietam (Sharpsburg) takes place.
September 18–19, 1862	General Lee leaves Maryland and enters Virginia.
September 22, 1862	President Lincoln issues the Preliminary Emancipation Proclamation.
October 1–5, 1862	President Lincoln travels to and visits General McClellan near Sharpsburg.
October 26, 1862	General McClellan crosses into Virginia in pursuit of General Lee.
November 5–7, 1862	President Lincoln relieves General McClellan of command, appointing Major General Ambrose Burnside as his replacement.

Chapter 1

ABRAHAM LINCOLN

"THE BOTTOM IS OUT OF THE TUB"

On January 10, 1862, President Lincoln voiced his frustration with the war to Quartermaster General Montgomery C. Meigs when he said, "The people are impatient; Chase has no money and he tells me he can raise no more; the General of the Army has typhoid fever. The bottom is out of the tub. What shall I do?"[3]

Chase was Secretary of the Treasury Salmon P. Chase. Lincoln's General of the Army was George B. McClellan. General McClellan had been delaying moving out of the Washington, D.C., area with the Army of the Potomac since assuming command in July 1861, after Major General Irvin McDowell's defeat at the First Battle of Bull Run. During these six months, McClellan reorganized, reequipped and trained his army. A frustrated Lincoln wondered if McClellan was going to "use" the Army of the Potomac; if not, Lincoln might want to borrow it.[4]

Newly named Secretary of War, Edwin Stanton had been a friend of McClellan's[5] when he took office in January 1862. As his experience with McClellan grew, Stanton developed little regard for McClellan, whom he considered an effective administrator but otherwise ineffective and "slow." Lincoln did not disagree with Stanton or other Republicans who also had little regard for the Democrat McClellan. Lincoln, however, believed that he had no alternatives.

Abraham Lincoln. *Library of Congress.*

Lincoln properly characterized that the bottom was out of the tub. Successes in the east were few in early 1862. General McDowell had failed at the first major battle of the war at Bull Run on July 21, 1861. A shocked Washington, D.C., watched the Union army and civilians who had gone to see the fight stream back into the city in a state of panic. Confederate General P.G.T. Beauregard and Thomas "Stonewall" Jackson pursued McDowell but stopped short of the capital. An ill-advised and poorly led battle at Ball's Bluff on October 21, 1861, resulted in a humiliating defeat of General McClelland's forces. Colonel Edward Baker, also a U.S. senator, was killed in the battle, leading to increased political unrest. The loss at Ball's Bluff led to the establishment of the Congressional Joint Committee on the Conduct of the War, which would review and criticize military action for the remainder of the war.[6] This commission would second-guess Lincoln and his generals with political zeal. With a significant number of Radical Republicans on the committee, McClellan was a frequent subject of their wrath.

The question of slavery and its role in the war and in Union politics had been a source of discussion and disagreement leading up to the war. President Lincoln had been considering the emancipation of slaves by the middle of the year. On July 22, 1862, he presented a first draft of his Emancipation Proclamation to his cabinet.[7] The proclamation was planned to go into effect on January 1, 1863. While the cabinet generally supported the proclamation, it received mixed opinions on when it should be issued. Secretary of War Stanton and Attorney General Edward Bates were in favor of immediate release. Treasury Secretary Salmon P. Chase was cool but supportive, while Secretary of the Interior Caleb B. Smith was the only member who opposed the Emancipation Proclamation. Secretary of State William Seward and Postmaster Montgomery Blair recommended waiting until a military victory to avoid the appearance of Union desperation. With the cabinet split, Lincoln took their positions under advisement.[8]

Successes in the west were evident but considered minor by the eastern establishment. Fort Donelson surrendered to General Ulysses S. Grant in February 1862, Pea Ridge in Arkansas was a Union success in March 1862 and Shiloh was another Grant victory in April 1862, despite suffering high Union casualties. That same month, Admiral David Farragut delivered New Orleans to the Union. An unimpeded Mississippi River remained as a major Union objective.

However, the war in the east continued to stall, causing Lincoln increased concern about the Army of the Potomac. Against his better judgement and the opinions of his cabinet, the Peninsula Campaign of General McClellan was approved in early 1862.[9] However, rather than giving McClellan total control, Lincoln retained enough troops under the command of General Irvin McDowell and, later, General John Pope to protect Washington, D.C. McClellan would later claim that the failure of his Peninsula Campaign was the result of the withholding of these troops. The campaign, with its goal of the capture of the Confederate capital of Richmond, finally started in early April 1862, after prodding by

President Lincoln and Secretary Stanton. The progress up the peninsula was conducted in a slow, methodical and purposeful manner by McClellan and included a questionable siege of Yorktown from April 3 to May 4, 1862. Confederate General Johnston did not understand why McClellan delayed an attack on Yorktown.[10] He reported to Richmond that McClellan could get through and around Yorktown anytime he wanted.[11] McClellan's movements can be attributed to the prevailing Union policy of conciliation and reunification. At this time, the Union wanted to coax the Confederacy back into the Union.

The Battle of Fair Oaks—or Seven Pines, as the Confederates called it—was fought on May 31. Despite McClellan's estimation of more than twice the actual number of Rebel forces facing his army, the Union was met by a clearly inferior number of Confederate troops. During the battle, Confederate General Joseph E. Johnston was severely wounded and was replaced by General Robert E. Lee, who began his storied command of the Army of Northern Virginia. The Battle of Fair Oaks marked the high-water mark of McClellan's Peninsula Campaign. Attacks by the Confederates in late June led to the Seven Days Battles between June 25 and July 1, culminating in the lone Union victory at Malvern Hill. After the retreat to Harrison's Landing, the campaign was considered and declared a failure by Lincoln when he visited McClellan on July 8. By early August, McClellan had been ordered to return to Washington.

The Confederacy, seeing the failure of the Union Peninsula Campaign and the Union retreat from the Confederate capital, turned its attention to the Union Army of Virginia, commanded by Major General John Pope. Pope, the egotistical western general disliked by his officers and enlisted men, was to be responsible for protecting Washington, D.C., during McClellan's absence. The poor estimation of Pope was a result of his arrogant pronouncement to the eastern troops on June 14, 1862.[12] As pressure from the Confederate army was placed on Pope, McClellan was ordered to move north toward Washington, D.C. On August 20, General Henry Halleck encouraged McClellan to rally all troops in support of General Pope.[13] McClellan was accused of delaying joining Pope on purpose. Major General Fitz John Porter's V Corps was present in support of Pope's forces for the battle. Arriving late, Porter fought a heavy battle on the Union left, opposing the forces of Longstreet and Jackson. Yet he was accused of disobeying Pope's orders to continue the attack. Porter was court-martialed and cashiered in November 1862. The battle, another win for the South, was a continued source of embarrassment to President Lincoln.

As a result of the defeat at Second Bull Run on August 28–30, 1862, General Pope was relieved of command. In spite of his reservations and the strong opposition by many in the Union government against his appointment, General McClellan was again named commander of all the forces in the Washington area in addition to his Army of the Potomac on September 2 by President Lincoln. General Pope was sent to command the Department of the Northwest to suppress the Sioux uprising in Minnesota. Major General McDowell, Pope's second in command, was without command for two years and then assigned to command the Department of the Pacific in San Francisco.

This, then, was the situation in the late summer of 1862 facing President Lincoln. There had been some successes in the west and nothing but military failure in the east, except for General Burnside's campaign in North Carolina. His eastern commander, General George B. McClellan, after the failed Peninsula Campaign, was mistrusted by Secretary Stanton and reluctantly given command of the reorganized Army of the Potomac by Lincoln. Some believe that the Peninsula Campaign could have been a victory had Lincoln not interceded. Nonetheless, there was no victory on the peninsula.

With the defense of Richmond and the defeat of General Pope at Bull Run, the Confederate Army of Northern Virginia and its commander, General Robert E. Lee, appeared invincible. The diary entry on September 6 by Union officer Marcena Pareic read, "There is a general feeling that the Southern Confederacy will be recognized & that they deserve to be recognized."[14]

The next few weeks and the performance of the Union army could seal the fate of the Union.

Chapter 2

George B. McClellan

Again, I have been called upon to save the country.[15]

Major General George Brinton McClellan, born on December 3, 1826, was second in his 1846 graduating class at West Point. Serving in the Mexican-American War, he left the U.S. Army in 1857. After a successful civilian career, he returned to the Union army in 1861 at the beginning of the Civil War. His experience as superintendent of two midwestern railroads demonstrated his skill as an excellent organizer. This background was first employed in organizing Ohio regiments at the beginning of the war.

His conservative views were based on the social and cultural values of the Whig Party, including discipline, hierarchy, moderation and enlightened reason. While retaining these values, he joined the Democratic Party in 1852.[16] McClellan had political objectives ever in his mind and understood that his military objectives were to achieve political goals.[17] This concept was outlined by Prussian General Carl von Clausewitz in *On War*.[18]

As he was a member of the Democratic Party, many of McClellan's opponents believed that he was proslavery and opposed to the war. Some went so far as to privately accuse him of failing to win battles on purpose. He expressed to his confidants a low opinion of President Lincoln and the Lincoln administration.

During his first campaign, in June 1861, he successfully defeated Confederate forces in western Virginia and won Union control of the area.

Major General George
B. McClellan. *Library of
Congress.*

He was considered the "Young Napoleon" by many and a winning general. After the Union loss at the First Battle of Bull Run, McClellan was named commander in August 1861, replacing General Irvin McDowell. He was also named General-in-Chief of the army on November 1, replacing General Winfield Scott upon his retirement.

McClellan, upon meeting an opposing force, consistently overestimated the strength of his military opponent. Often, he estimated Confederate strength at twice its actual strength. His cavalry commander, Brigadier General Alfred Pleasonton, and civilian intelligence chief, Allan Pinkerton, provided inflated enemy estimates throughout McClellan's tenure. Bruce Catton, in *Mr. Lincoln's Army*, characterized Pinkerton thusly: "He had energy, courage, administrative ability, and imagination—too much imagination."[19] Some, including historian Joseph L. Harsh, believe that McClellan's troop estimates were for all troops in the theater who could be brought into action, thus justifying the overestimation.[20] In McClellan's defense, overestimation of enemy strength was also done by General Halleck, Governor Curtis of

Pennsylvania and many newspaper reports.[21] As a result of McClellan's estimates and his unwillingness to place his army at risk, he was consistently reluctant to engage the enemy. Known by the Lincoln administration for his inaction, he was constantly pressed by Secretary Stanton, President Lincoln and army Chief of Staff Major General Henry Halleck to take action.

Reporting that the Army of the Potomac was in a very poor state of training, equipment and morale, McClellan spent from July 1861 until April 1862 refitting and training the army. Only at the insistence of Secretary Stanton and President Lincoln did General McClellan begin executing his Peninsula Campaign. This campaign was planned by McClellan and reluctantly approved by President Lincoln. Prior to the campaign, on March 11, President Lincoln relieved McClellan of his General-in-Chief duties and assumed them himself.

Beginning in April 1862, the Army of the Potomac, under the command of McClellan, moved to Fort Monroe at the James River, slowly moving up the peninsula toward Richmond with about 100,000 troops. Much to McClellan's displeasure, President Lincoln had created the Army of Virginia from McDowell's command with 38,000 Union troops to protect the Washington, D.C., and assigned command to General John Pope. Lincoln called on McClellan's corps commanders to assess, without McClellan's input, the need for troops to protect Washington.[22] Seen as micromanagement by Lincoln, this confirmed McClellan's low opinion of his Commander-in-Chief. The increased number of troops withheld from McClellan was based on Lincoln's analysis that McClellan had initially failed to provide adequate protection for Washington, D.C. McClellan claimed that he had provided 73,000 troops, while Lincoln counted only 29,000. McClellan had twice counted some troops and included General Banks's command in the Shenandoah Valley.[23] Lincoln responded to McClellan's complaint of withholding troops from his command with, "You now have 100,000 troops with you."[24] Shortly after his departure to the peninsula, McClellan was notified that McDowell's Corps would be diverted to protect Washington.[25]

While McClellan resented the loss of troops to McDowell, the aggressive action of "Stonewall" Jackson in the Shenandoah Valley against the inept Union Generals Nathaniel P. Banks and John C. Frémont justified the withholding of these forces. Jackson's primary victory took place at Winchester on May 23, when he routed Banks, driving him across the Potomac into Maryland.[26] Initially, General McDowell was to support McClellan to the north as McClellan approached Richmond from the east.

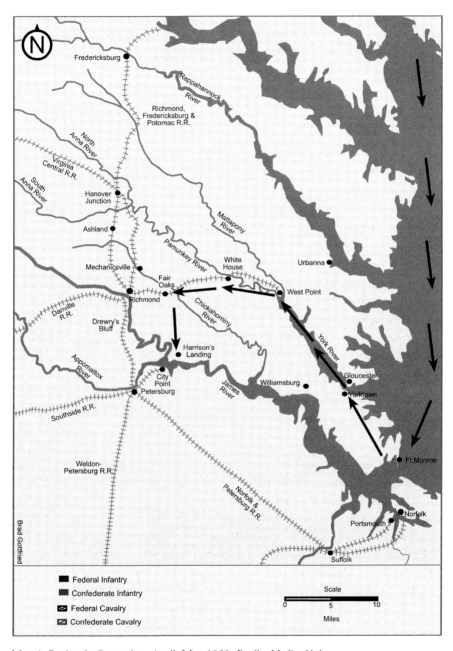

Map 1. Peninsula Campaign, April–May 1862. *Bradley M. Gottfried.*

By late May, however, McClellan had realized that McDowell's promised support would not to be provided.[27]

After the Siege of Yorktown in early May, McClellan began slowly pursuing Confederate Generals James Longstreet and D.H. Hill toward Richmond, the seat of the Confederate government. Accepting estimates of an enemy force of 120,000 men (nearly double the actual Confederate strength), McClellan hesitated within sight of the church steeples of Richmond.

The investment of Richmond by McClellan would continue until General "Stonewall" Jackson returned from operations in the Shenandoah Valley. Jackson added about 18,000 troops to Lee, bringing the total to 86,000 men, still short of McClellan's strength. General Johnston knew that General McDowell was poised north of Richmond to support McClellan. If McDowell could join with McClellan, Johnston would face a three-to-one manpower disadvantage. Rather than face this, Johnston's decision was to attack.[28] On May 24, President Lincoln assured McClellan that McDowell would head south to assist him. Shortly after, McDowell's march was suspended, and he was sent to the Shenandoah Valley to challenge Jackson.[29]

On May 31, the Confederates attacked the split Union forces on the north shore of the Chickahominy River at Fair Oaks. Without McDowell, as promised by President Lincoln, McClellan's right flank was dangerously in the air. McClellan had planned the deployment of his troops on the assumption that McDowell would be available to protect his right flank. The lack of support from McDowell was a critical component to the success of Johnston's attack. Even if McDowell had been available, it is unlikely McClellan would have assaulted Richmond. He had planned to bring up heavy artillery and begin a siege. He was aware that he had insufficient forces to storm Richmond.[30]

The army corps—commanded by Major General Fitz John Porter, Major General William Franklin and Major General Edwin Sumner on the north side of the river—were attacked by Confederate Generals A.P. Hill and John Magruder. The remainder of McClellan's forces and his headquarters were on the opposite side. Under normal circumstances, the Chickahominy was a slow-moving stream easily crossed on bridges or by fording, allowing McClellan to move troops across the river in support of the north side. However, heavy and continuous rains had swelled the river and imperiled the bridges.[31]

The battle was inconclusive. Confederate troops were commanded by inexperienced officers, and less than half of Johnston's army entered the fighting. Limited roads, swamps and forests where little or no reconnaissance was conducted further hampered the Confederates. Poor command and difficult conditions would plague the Confederate army throughout the Peninsula Campaign.

Of chief significance during the Battle of Seven Pines, General Robert E. Lee assumed command of Confederate forces shortly after the wounding of General Joseph Johnston. General McClellan reported that he preferred Lee to Johnston, as Lee was too cautious and weak in his responsibility. Later, McClellan realized that he had misjudged Lee, who was neither cautious nor weak.[32]

During most of June, McClellan communicated with Secretary Stanton reporting his inability to move because of poor weather and even reported that General P.G.T. Beauregard had arrived in the area with his troops.[33] Beauregard had just commanded at the Siege of Corinth, Mississippi, and arrived in distant Charleston, South Carolina, on May 31, 1862.

Confederate forces attacked the Union at Mechanicsville on June 26, 1862, marking the beginning of the Seven Days Battles. General McClellan's retreat—or, as he referred to the action, as changing his base—was marked by pitched battles in which Lee's outmanned Rebels forced the Union to continue to fall back. Lee, however, failed to order his cavalry to reconnoiter McClellan's retreating forces and lost much of the advantage of offensive pressure.

Mechanicsville was inconclusive, with Porter repulsing A.P. Hill at Beaver Dam Creek, while "Stonewall" Jackson arrived too late to be effective. After McClellan was delayed in the morass of White Oak Swamp, Magruder attacked McClellan's rear guard at Savage's Station. His attack was stopped for lack of support by Jackson. On June 30, Lee planned a flank attack at Frayser's Farm. This failed, again due to the tardy performance of "Stonewall" Jackson. July 1, 1862, ended the retrograde with the Battle of Malvern Hill, where the Union held off the exhausted Confederates. General Lee had misjudged the strength of Union defenses, especially the large artillery presence, and attacked with disastrous results. Except for Malvern Hill, General McClellan had been out-generaled (although he inflicted greater casualties on the Confederates) in the campaign that he had carefully planned to defeat the Confederacy. On June 26, McClellan had been within five miles of Richmond. On July 2, he was at Harrison's Landing, twenty miles from Richmond. Some supporters of McClellan submit that his movement of his base to Harrison's Landing was done on purpose. The movement to the security and logistic support of the James, while inflicting greater damage on the Confederacy than on itself, was a

Major General J.E.B. Stuart.
Library of Congress.

victory for the Union. Excluding the heavy losses by the Confederacy at Malvern Hill, losses on both sides were about equal. Without the additional forces that he indicated he needed, and Washington refused to provide, the relocation of his base appears more like a retreat.[34] To add insult to the defeat on the peninsula on June 13–15, Confederate cavalry under J.E.B. Stuart successfully rode around the entire Union army, capturing 170 prisoners and 300 horses, while suffering only the loss of a single trooper.

Completing his movement to Harrison's Landing, McClellan had warships of the Union navy to protect his troops. His lines of communication for logistic support were virtually unlimited thanks to the control of inland waters by the Union. General Lee realized that attacking McClellan at Harrison's Landing was undesirable. He, however, could take pride in driving a superior force from Richmond. McClellan believed that he could reestablish his initiative if he could receive 50,000 additional troops. Lincoln responded, "I have not seventy-five thousand men east of the mountains."[35]

At a meeting with President Lincoln at Harrison's Landing on July 8, 1862, McClellan delivered a letter to the president outlining his "general views concerning the existing state of the rebellion."[36] Lincoln did not visit McClellan to discuss the general's views on conducting the war.[37] He was interested in why the campaign was a failure and how the campaign could be terminated and troops could be returned north. On July 11, 1862, President Lincoln appointed General Henry Halleck General-in-Chief of the Union army, a subtle repudiation of General McClellan. Halleck visited McClellan on July 25, offering 20,000 reinforcements for a renewal of the attack on Richmond, bringing his forces to 110,000. McClellan estimated 200,000 Confederates defending Richmond. No action was taken on this offer.[38] Lincoln believed that McClellan would not fight and that the campaign should be terminated.[39]

McClellan received orders on August 3 to return to Washington. After the Peninsula Campaign and actions by the Confederates in the Shenandoah Valley, Lincoln had reservations about the tactic of operating against Richmond.[40]

McClellan's Peninsula Campaign was characterized by ponderous movement, questionable tactical decisions, timidity and constant overestimation of enemy strength. Finally, McClellan blamed his Commander-in-Chief, President Lincoln, for his failure. As the campaign wound down, McClellan wired Secretary Stanton, "I have lost this battle because my force was too small." He continued, "[T]he Government must not and cannot hold me responsible for the result." Finally, "I tell you plainly that I owe no thanks to you or to any other person in Washington."[41] McClellan was fortunate that the last two lines of the comment were deleted when the message was decoded. Lincoln and Stanton saw that portion of the message well after the event.[42] McClellan's complaint had some merit, as the campaign in front of Richmond was planned with the troops from General McDowell available to support McClellan. However, to blame the administration for the loss gained him no supporters in Washington.

After August 3, 1862, General McClellan began moving troops north as directed. His movement north proceeded smoothly and efficiently.[43] From the Confederate perspective, Richmond was safe, thanks to the heroic action of the Confederate army and its new leader, General Lee, who could now turn his attention to General Pope on the Rappahannock River. McClellan was expected to provide support to General Pope. McClellan attributed his delay in supporting Pope to the condition of his army, inadequate material and the lack of transportation. He categorized his army as "thoroughly exhausted and depleted by its desperate fighting and severe marches in the unhealthy regions of the Chickahominy."[44] In addition to General Porter,

Pope ultimately was reinforced by only a portion of two corps from the Army of the Potomac on August 29–30, 1862, at the Second Battle of Bull Run.

General McClellan's initial troops, commanded by General Fitz John Porter, joined Pope on August 26, 1862;[45] however, they initially participated in the operation but were too few in number to change the course of the battle. Upon the arrival of Longstreet, Porter refused orders from Pope to attack.[46] Troops from Generals Franklin and Sumner arrived too late to support Pope. General McClellan had waited until August 28 to order General Franklin forward to support Pope. McClellan throughout the battle was located at Alexandria, clearly within supporting distance of Pope.[47] McClellan provided no other support to Pope and on August 29 halted the movement of Franklin.

Pope was attacked, outmaneuvered, out-generaled and defeated at the Second Battle of Bull Run. Lee showed bold maneuvering during the battle. As a precursor of future action, he split his forces, sending Jackson on a long march around the right flank of Pope, and then defeated a disorganized and confused Pope at the old site of the First Battle of Bull Run. As a result of the defeat, General Pope was cashiered, and on September 2 General McClellan was named commander of his reorganized Army of the Potomac, with the addition of the Army of Virginia and troops in the Washington area. In spite of criticism from Lincoln, his administration and other Republicans of McClellan's shortcomings, many military leaders spoke highly of his leadership. Even those who criticized him gave him credit for developing an inefficient army, garnering the support of his troops. Other supporters pointed out that McClellan was a victim of extensive political intrigue and noted that he fought the Confederate army at its military peak. McClellan organized the consolidated command, the Army of the Potomac, into three sub-commands or wings under Major Generals Ambrose Burnside, Edwin Sumner and William Franklin.

McClellan's former position of General-in-Chief of the army was handed to General Henry Halleck. This move was made by Lincoln because when McClellan was in the General-in-Chief position, nothing happened.[48] Halleck, known (not affectionately) as "Old Brains,"[49] graduated third in his West Point class of 1839. He published *Elements of Military Art and Science* in 1846, which became the basic tactical publication of the Civil War. As commander of the Western Theater, Halleck was not directly involved in any western victories, including those of General U.S. Grant. Taking field command for the Siege of Corinth, he was known for extreme caution. McClellan had a low opinion of Halleck. In his autobiography, McClellan stated, "Halleck was the most hopelessly stupid. It was more difficult to get an idea through his head than can be conceived by anyone who ever made the attempt."[50] Halleck and McClellan detested each other, first crossing swords with McClellan as General-in-Chief in the fall of 1861 when Halleck was in command of troops in the west. Halleck disagreed strongly with McClellan's approach to the war in the west. Halleck believed that McClellan had little use for the river system in the west and was tied to road transportation. This early conflict contributed to ongoing tension between the two.[51]

Major General Henry Halleck. *Library of Congress.*

On September 4, 1862, General Lee began his invasion of the North. General George B. McClellan was responsible for the pursuit of General Lee and the Army of Northern Virginia into Maryland. General McClellan had the following campaign objectives as he departed the Washington area: (1) Protect Washington and Baltimore from Confederate attack; (2) Prohibit General Lee from successfully moving Confederate troops into Pennsylvania; and (3) Force General Lee back into Virginia. The concept of destroying the enemy army had yet to become an objective of the Union. During 1861 and into 1862, conciliation and pressuring the Confederacy to abandon its separation through military action was the objective of the Union.

General George B. McClellan's Army of the Potomac was destined to meet the Army of Northern Virginia, under General Robert E. Lee, in one of the greatest military engagements in United States history.

Chapter 3

Robert E. Lee

"General are you going to send us in again?"…
"Yes, my son, you all must do what you can."[52]

Robert E. Lee, born in 1807, was a graduate of West Point in 1829, ranking second in his class. Lee was a captain on the staff of Lieutenant General Winfield Scott during the Mexican-American War (1846–48), serving with distinction.

Lee served as Superintendent of West Point beginning in 1852. Appointed lieutenant colonel of the 2nd Cavalry in 1855, Lee was headquartered in Jefferson Barracks in Missouri. In October 1859, he was assigned to suppress the slave insurrection of John Brown at Harper's Ferry. He was then assigned as commander of the Department of Texas in 1860.

At the outbreak of the Civil War, Lee was offered, by General Scott, command of the Union army being formed to fight the Confederate insurrection. While he opposed secession, he said he could not take part in action against his home state of Virginia, where he was offered command of its troops. As a result, Lee resigned his commission and reported to Richmond in April 1861.

General Lee believed that it was necessary for the Confederacy to aggressively attack the Union to reduce the length of the war. If the war was prolonged, the lack of strength of the Confederate army would become a problem for the South. This view was contrary to that of President Jefferson

Robert E. Lee. *Library of Congress.*

Davis, who favored a guerrilla-style war to wear down the Union, leading to recognition of the Confederacy. Prussian General Carl von Clausewitz, in his famous treatise on war in 1832, postulated that the leading principle of war was the destruction of the enemy's military force.[53] Clausewitz further stated that war does not consist of a single instantaneous blow. Destruction of the enemy could be by military means or by destroying the enemy's will to win. Clausewitz used the following example:

> *Fredrick the great, during the Seven Years' War was never strong enough to overthrow the Austrian monarchy; and if he had tried to do so after the fashion of Charles the Twelfth, he would have inevitably have had to succumb himself. But after his skillful application of the system of*

husbanding his resources had shown the powers allied against him, through the seven years' struggle, that the actual expenditure of strength far exceeded what they had first anticipated, they made peace.[54]

While Lee understood the principle of defeating the enemy, he failed to understand, as Davis understood, that defeating the enemy included defeating the enemy's will to fight.

President Jefferson Davis acted as Commander-in-Chief of the army, subordinating army generals to lesser roles. General Lee, after assignment to a variety of insignificant roles, was named chief advisor to President Davis in July 1861. On June 1, 1862, General Lee was, with Davis's reservations, given command of the Army of Northern

President Jefferson Davis. *Library of Congress.*

Virginia, after its commander, General Joseph Johnston, was wounded at Fair Oaks, Virginia, attacking General McClellan. The elevation of Lee to high command was not a given. President Davis had been visiting the Army of Northern Virginia for several days. Lee, as Davis's military advisor, accompanied the president. Davis had concern about Lee's ability to command a large army. He properly noted that General Lee had little command experience, operating primarily as staff officer. After more than thirty years of experience in the army, Lee did most of his work as an engineer on rivers, ports and harbors. Nevertheless, upon Johnston's incapacity, Davis turned to Robert E. Lee to command the Army of Northern Virginia. Part of Lee's early success was that he knew Davis and communicated well with him.

Lee accepted his limited command and the presence of an unknown and largely ineffective staff. As a result, he put great faith in four veteran commanders. Major Generals "Stonewall" Jackson, James Longstreet, D.H. Hill and A.P. Hill were given wide latitude, with simple orders provided by Lee. These generals were expected to flesh out these orders and coordinate, as needed, with other officers. J.E.B. Stuart was given responsibility to

Left: Major General James Longstreet. *Right*: Major General Thomas "Stonewall" Jackson. *Library of Congress.*

provide reconnaissance of McClellan's army. Unfortunately, as later seen at Antietam, Stuart found raiding more to his liking. Frequently, Lee did not know the location of his subordinate commanders and was required to assume that they would implement his vague orders.

General Lee, along with his trusted Major Generals James Longstreet and "Stonewall" Jackson, began aggressively taking offensive action against General McClellan between June and July during McClellan's retreat from Richmond. At this time, Lee out-generaled McClellan. Lee's successes were not without problems. Usually dependable, "Stonewall" Jackson was tardy for attacks on four occasions, including engagements at Beaver Dam Creek and Savage's Station. The flank attack at Frayser's Farm was stopped because of Jackson's delay. At Malvern Hill on June 1, 1862, General Lee unwisely chose to attack General McClellan in well-fortified and defended positions. His attack was repelled with significant losses to the Confederacy. General Lee withdrew his forces, satisfied that he had driven the Union forces from Richmond. With significantly fewer troops available to Lee compared to McClellan, Lee's forces fought effectively and never allowed McClellan to gain the initiative. Despite significant shortcomings, Lee had driven McClellan from Richmond.

Lee's first combat command was a tactical success but lacked military efficiency.[55] Strong-willed subordinates who were given wide latitude would

Left: Major General A.P. Hill. *Right*: Major General D.H. Hill. *Library of Congress.*

provide Lee with challenges he had never encountered during his days as a staff officer. General Lee was a mediator rather than a strong command-oriented leader. He expected to civilly gain conformity and cooperation from Jackson, Longstreet, A.P. Hill and D.H. Hill through a quiet, suggestive and conciliatory tone. This would be a challenge to the general through his time as commander of the Army of Northern Virginia. General Jackson continued to effectively operate, essentially, as a separate command responding to Lee's orders in his own way. Cavalry commander General J.E.B. Stuart would also provide command challenges to Lee.

Having been satisfied that McClellan was no longer a threat to Richmond and the Confederate army, General Lee turned his attention to General John Pope, who commanded nearly 38,000 Union troops in the vicinity of Bull Run. In spite of the risk, Lee dangerously divided his troops, sending "Stonewall" Jackson on a sixty-two-mile marching envelopment around the right of Pope's army in forty-eight hours, attacking the Union supply depot at Manassas Junction.

Upon realizing that Jackson was at Manassas Junction in his rear, Pope was determined to find and defeat Jackson before Lee could bring all his 55,000 troops together. Unfortunately, without Pope knowing, Jackson had moved to a wooded ridge a few miles west of the old Manassas battlefield.

Pope's small and overworked cavalry was unable to immediately locate the slippery Jackson. On the afternoon of August 28, a brigade commanded by Brigadier General John Gibbon, consisting of troops from Wisconsin and Indiana, stumbled on Jackson's position, resulting in a sharp firefight. The "Iron Brigade of the West" soon earned its reputation as one of the best units in the army. In the meantime, the remainder of Lee's forces under General Longstreet attacked the left flank of the Union to relieve the pressure on Jackson. Pope's men withdrew to the site to the west and ultimately retreated on August 30–31.

General Lee defeated Pope at the Second Battle of Bull Run using superior tactical movement of Confederate forces against a confused opponent. During this campaign, Lee's instructions to his commanders were frequently verbal and undocumented. This method of command was to be repeated throughout his time in command of the Army of Northern Virginia.

Lee's army had been marching almost continuously for ten weeks, and the men were ragged and hungry; yet after another win for the Army of Northern Virginia, Lee could look for new opportunities to attack the Union. General Lee believed that invading the North could produce several positive effects. First, whatever he would do, the demoralized Union command could not compete with the Confederates. Successful invasion would rally Southern sympathy in Maryland and result in significant recruiting for the Confederate army.[56] Lee's proclamation to the people of Maryland, issued on September 8, 1862 (see Appendix 3), outlines this objective. Attacking targets in Maryland and Pennsylvania, Lee believed, would have a devastating impact on Northern morale and, perhaps, lead to negotiations with the South. At least, Lee thought, the invasion would influence the November Congressional elections in the North. Lee knew that every day his army could spend in Pennsylvania would provide positive support for the election of Peace Democrats in the fall election.

President Lincoln was working with his own party split between conservative and radical factions. The Democrats were likewise split between the Peace and War Democrats, along with the Provisional War Democrats, and Lincoln needed the Democrats to support his volunteer raising of the army to fight the rebellion.[57] Increased election of Peace Democrats in the 1862 election could have a critical impact on troop recruiting. The presence of Rebel forces in Maryland and Pennsylvania could result in greater acceptance of Peace Democratic candidates and increased pressure to negotiate with the Confederacy.

General Lee reported his intentions of invading Pennsylvania in communications with President Davis on September 3, 1862, in which he stated, "I propose to enter Pennsylvania, unless you should deem it unadvisable upon political or other grounds."[58] The Confederate army's mere presence in the North was more important to the South than any military victory that might be achieved. This invasion could also lead to recognition of the political legitimacy of the Confederacy by England and France. Lee believed that this recognition was critical to the long-term success of the Confederacy. The decision to attack in the North was part of the Confederacy's strategic plan for winning the war. President Davis shared Lee's position on the invasion and the importance of European recognition of the Confederate states.

With President Davis's approval of the Northern invasion, General Lee was buoyed by his recent successes, as well as a belief that he not only understood the limitations of General McClellan but also had confidence in his plan for the invasion of Maryland. Just when the elevation of McClellan as the commander of Union forces replacing General Pope was made known to Lee is lost in history. Lee's plan for movement north was expected to be effective if Pope or McClellan were in command of the opposing forces. On September 4, 1862, General Lee began a critical phase in the war: an invasion of the North. This invasion resulted in a critical clash between General Lee and General McClellan in the fields, orchards and woods near the quiet farm town of Sharpsburg, Maryland, overlooking the sluggish Antietam Creek. This meeting, on the bloodiest day in American history, was to be a pivotal point in the Civil War.

Chapter 4

PRELUDE TO ANTIETAM

To President Lincoln, the bottom was surely out of the tub. Continued losses by General McClellan and the Army of the Potomac and the embarrassing defeat at the Second Battle of Bull Run haunted Lincoln. The successes in the west by General Grant had slowed but were of some consolation. Attempts to capture Vicksburg and open the Mississippi River to Union control had been unsuccessful, with the gunboats of Admiral Farragut blasting Vicksburg. Even with the western successes, to the Washington politicians, this was of interest but too far away to offset the concerns in the east. After all, to many politicians, the east was where the war would be won or lost. The ultimate control of the Mississippi River and its tributaries had a huge impact on the ability of the Confederacy to remain viable. The Tennessee, Cumberland, Duck and Mississippi Rivers, when controlled by the North, provided excellent lines of communication for movement south by Union forces west of the Allegheny Mountains and limited movement west by Confederate forces to support the Western Theater. This, coupled with the limited railroad branches in the South running east and west beyond the mountains, split the Confederacy in two, giving great east/west capabilities to the North.

Lincoln had been contemplating issuing an Emancipation Proclamation since mid-1862. On July 17, 1862, Congress passed the Second Confiscation Act, which included the freeing of all slaves in Federally controlled areas. President Lincoln wanted to provide implementation of the Congressional act as army Commander-in-Chief by the issuance of his own proclamation.

A draft was discussed with his cabinet, which was concerned about the timing of the release of the proclamation. After further consideration, President Lincoln deferred the announcement until a Union military victory.[59] Based on the current military situation, Lincoln's issue of his Emancipation Proclamation would have to wait until the fall of 1862, when the military victory at Antietam was achieved.

Republicans and Democrats were critical of Lincoln and his cabinet, as well as the continued dependence on General McClellan to defeat General Lee and the Confederacy. Pressure by General Lee on Washington, D.C., and Baltimore and threats to Pennsylvania worried everyone. Failure to protect the important center of the Union was blamed on the president and his generals. Washington was apprehensive about the safety of the capital and concerned that both the capital and Baltimore were vulnerable to occupation by the Confederacy.

The population and politicians in Maryland and Pennsylvania were concerned for their safety after news of General Lee's Army of Northern Virginia's movement across the Potomac. Militias were called to duty, assets were moved for protection and the population prepared for the invasion. The people of Union-supporting Maryland and Pennsylvania looked south with concern and apprehension. The worried population of Washington and Baltimore expected General McClellan to cover and protect their cities.

In the Confederacy, successes in the east led to a belief that their cause was just and their future bright—with General Lee's leadership, they would surely prevail. The Army of Northern Virginia was strong and prepared for more action. It was only a matter of time before the Union would be brought to its knees and would petition to end the war. The powers of Europe would follow, recognizing the Confederacy. General Lee would lead the South to a magnificent victory.

In Europe, economists watched, with interest, the possible bankruptcy of the Union. The cost of the American Civil War appeared to be bringing the United States to ruin. England was sympathetic to the Confederate cause but had difficulty reconciling the institution of slavery. Indeed, a major point of contention in Europe was the existence of slavery in the Confederacy. Slave trade had been outlawed in Great Britain in 1807 and in France in 1830. Many in both countries objected to the support of the South based solely on the slavery issue.

Great Britain maintained a position of strict neutrality, even though a split North America was to its advantage. Louis Napoleon III of France asked England to cooperate in the recognition of the Confederacy and breaking of the Union blockade. British Prime Minister Lord Palmerston refused to interfere, only for the sake of the availability of cotton. He suggested England mediate the dispute between the North and South. The Lincoln administration strongly opposed this action by Britain. Among other problems with such negotiations, the Union would be required to acknowledge the legitimacy of the Confederacy, which Lincoln would not do. The conflict between the United States and England was further strained on November 8, 1861, by the boarding and seizure by the United States of the British mail packet *Trent*, carrying Confederate diplomats James M. Madison and John Slidell on a mission of the Confederacy to Great Britain. President Lincoln avoided conflict with Great Britain on January 14, 1862, when Madison and Slidell were released, and the Trent Affair ended. However, the relationship between the Union and England continued to be strained. England desired Southern cotton to meet the demand for its products. This was the primary opportunity for the Confederacy to seek recognition by Great Britain. Softening of overall cotton demand by English mills and the availability of Egyptian cotton mitigated the Southern influence on British policy. Still, Southern cotton was needed to keep British mills working.

General McClellan was still reeling from his loss on the peninsula. However, blaming others, especially Lincoln, for withholding troops for the defense of Washington, D.C., and being chosen to replace General Pope to again save the nation, he retained his confidence. McClellan looked forward to the challenge of stopping General Lee's invasion of the North. President Lincoln and Secretary Stanton, being forced to commit to General McClellan, were guardedly optimistic that McClellan would rise to the challenge. General Burnside had refused to take command of the Army of the Potomac, Generals Pope and McDowell had been failures and other generals in the Eastern Theater were unknown and untried. While both Stanton and Lincoln had reservations about McClellan, there appeared to be little choice in command. There was no one else who had the qualifications to command a large army. General Lee had clear objectives for the invasion of Maryland and was filled with confidence from recent successes. Jefferson Davis had unlimited confidence in General Lee and was awaiting reports of success from the field.

Great Britain and France were reading dispatches from America as they evaluated their position on the Confederacy and the Union. With the events unfolding in Maryland being watched by all, whichever side prevailed would reap significant dividends. Little did anyone know the cost of the great battle that was about to take place in the cornfields, orchards and woods of Maryland.

Chapter 5

MOVEMENT TO ANTIETAM

Geneeral Lee crossed into Maryland on September 4, 1862, with an estimated 55,000 troops,[60] including three divisions of reinforcements sent from Richmond. Despite Lee's belief that he would be received as a conquering hero, his reception in Maryland was cool. The ragged, poorly shod Confederate troops provided little confidence for their cause. On September 7, Lee reported to Jefferson Davis that he did not expect significant recruiting.[61] It is estimated at that time that no more than 200 Marylanders joined the rebellion. For the second time since assuming command, General Lee violated a principle of command by confidently splitting his forces in the face of the enemy. He first split his forces at the Second Battle of Bull Run to allow General Jackson to ride around the right flank of Pope and at Antietam to engage Harper's Ferry while preparing to proceed into Pennsylvania. General Lee issued Special Orders No. 191 on September 9, 1862 (see Appendix 2). Beginning at Frederick, Maryland, he sent "Stonewall" Jackson on a round-about route to Harper's Ferry via Boonsboro, Sharpsburg and Martinsburg. (Special Orders No. 191 called for Jackson to move via Sharpsburg; however, Jackson chose to go on a longer route through Williamsport to engage Union forces there, delaying the timing of Lee's invasion.) The divisions of General John Walker and General Lafayette McLaws of Longstreet's command were sent to Harper's Ferry via shorter routes—McLaws through Crampton's Gap in South Mountain to Pleasant Valley approaching Maryland Heights north of Harper's Ferry and Walker south across the Potomac River, occupying

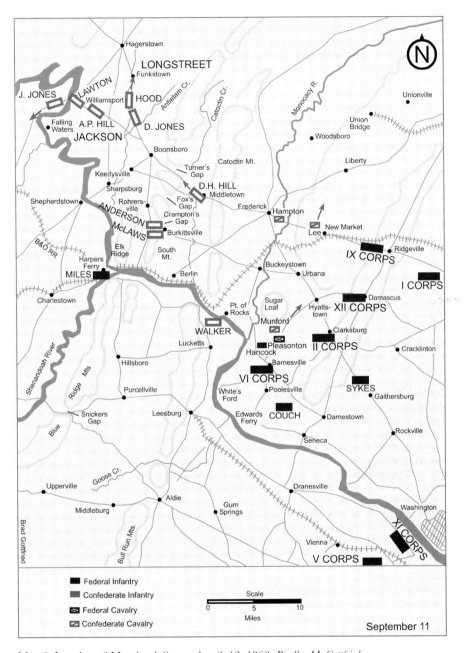

Map 2. Invasion of Maryland, September 2–13, 1862. *Bradley M. Gottfried.*

Boonsboro, Maryland. *Library of Congress.*

Loudoun Heights south of Harper's Ferry. "Stonewall" Jackson was then to invest Harper's Ferry from Bolivar Heights to the west. General Longstreet was opposed to the Harper's Ferry program as "not worth the game."[62] This claim was made well after the war with no basis. Nevertheless, he supported the decision by General Lee to invest and capture Harper's Ferry in the face of an approaching Union army.

As the possible engagement with the Union developed, the remainder of Longstreet's command, along with General Lee, moved toward Hagerstown from Boonsboro, followed by General D.H. Hill from Jackson's command as rear guard. Hill was forced to retrace his movement to defend Turner's and Fox's Gaps in South Mountain as General McClellan's forces approached. The cavalry of J.E.B. Stuart provided a squadron each for Longstreet, Jackson and McLaws. The remainder, along with Lee's trains, followed Longstreet. Hagerstown was the logical place for Lee to establish his headquarters, as it was the best location for movement into Pennsylvania. Lee's ultimate location of his troops in Sharpsburg was not his primary or even secondary objective. Circumstances at South Mountain caused Lee to change his plans for the invasion.

By September 3, 1862, General Henry Halleck had received information that General Lee was preparing to make a raid on Maryland.[63] On September 7, General McClellan moved his headquarters to the field at Rockville, Maryland, where he remained for four days while his troops moved toward Frederick. Union movement into Maryland reflected McClellan's Whig outlook—advance deliberately, orderly and methodically[64]—with McClellan concerned about protecting Washington and Baltimore from the Confederate troops. Some of the excessive caution of McClellan may have been a result of Allen Pinkerton's August 10 intelligence analysis that Confederate manpower in Virginia was 200,000, with 120,000 troops threatening Washington, D.C. Estimates of total Confederate strength entering Maryland ranged from more than 100,000 crossing the Potomac River from General Alfred Pleasonton's cavalry and early reports of 75,000 Rebels in Frederick,

Brigadier General Alfred Pleasonton. *Library of Congress.*

Maryland, which represented about one-third of the Confederate forces. The arithmetic on the size of Lee's forces does not support the Pinkerton and Pleasonton numbers. Accepted numbers of Confederate troops around Richmond in the summer of 1862 was under 115,000. After losses during the Peninsula Campaign and Second Battle of Bull Run and allowing for the troops remaining around Richmond, Lee could have moved to Maryland, at most, with only half the original strength.[65] Also, McClellan had a good idea of the number of units facing him, based on "commands" identified in Special Orders No. 191.[66] At the Second Battle of Bull Run, Confederate commands, or wings, known to the Union, consisted of three divisions. Had McClellan changed "command" in the Special Orders to "wings," he could have closely estimated Lee's strength.[67] Pinkerton and Pleasonton, could have estimated that no more than 160 regiments were with Lee. The strength of Union regiments was approximately 50 percent of the authorized level of 1,000 men. There is no reason to believe that the Army of Northern Virginia would have available for duty an excess of the Union army's level. Even with this conservative estimate of 80,000 troops, the number was substantially less than the lowest Union intelligence estimates of 100,000. Using McClellan's estimate of 120,000 Rebels facing him, the Confederate forces facing him at South Mountain would have been substantially less. Special Orders No. 191 clearly indicated that two-thirds of Lee's forces would be at Harper's Ferry, leaving only 40,000 facing McClellan at South Mountain. When Lee began his march north, he did so in full view of the Union signal station at Sugarloaf Mountain.[68] On the afternoon of September 4, the station reported Lee's movement to Washington. Based on the observation from the station, it is likely that the estimate of Lee's strength should have been substantially less than the estimates of Pinkerton and Pleasonton.[69] Edwin C. Fishel, a foremost student of McClellan intelligence capabilities, has stated that "the ultimate sources were guesswork and rumor."[70]

Another significant part of McClellan's movement, including General Burnside moving his wing primarily north rather than west toward Lee's forces, was McClellan's objective of protecting Washington and Baltimore from Confederate attack. This shift north, as well as west, provided this protection. Burnside was a close confidant of McClellan's and was the only general in McClellan's command who had experience in commanding a large army. It was logical for Burnside to be responsible for this important assignment. On September 9, 1862, McClellan's army, except for some cavalry, was still twenty-five miles southeast of Frederick, Maryland, and after two days of marching covered only about eleven miles. McClellan's organization of his army into three wings allowed movement over three routes rather than following one unit after another. He was now moving along three routes: Burnside's wing was on the right moving through Brookville to the National Road, Sumner in the center through Rockville and Urbana and Franklin on the left, north of the Chesapeake and Ohio Canal toward Buckeystown. Roads on these routes were generally good by Civil War standards, and since the weather had been good, the roads were dry. McClellan was faced with natural barriers between his army and the Confederates. The first was Parr's Ridge, then west to the Monocacy River near Frederick and Catoctin Mountain. West of there was the imposing South Mountain, followed by Pleasant Valley and Elk Ridge, frequently referred to as "Elk Mountain" in official reports, as well as the Cumberland Valley. McClellan knew that the Confederates were west of South Mountain and the three gaps leading beyond the mountain. All the while, McClellan, who believed that he was outnumbered, continued to protect Washington and Baltimore from attack. He knew the approximate location of the Confederate forces before he received the Lost Orders and could begin an attack at any time.

At this time, the 14,000 Union men at Harper's Ferry were hopelessly surrounded, with Confederate troops on high ground on all sides. On September 5, 1862, the garrison at Harper's Ferry was ordered not to abandon the facility. General McClellan had recommended that the 10,400 men at Harper's Ferry and 2,500 troops at Martinsburg be evacuated and placed under his command. General Halleck refused, thus sealing the fates of these troops. The refusal to abandon Harper's Ferry was significant in delaying Lee's movement north. The isolation of Harper's Ferry gave General Lee renewed confidence that it could be easily captured, and the large quantity of arms could be in Confederate hands. Further, control of Harper's Ferry was critical to Lee's plans for the invasion of Pennsylvania. The existence of the large Union force at Harper's Ferry was a significant risk of interference or interruption to Lee's logistic lifeline through the Shenandoah Valley. While Lee believed that Harper's Ferry would fall easily, easy or difficult, it must fall.

On September 11, General McClellan had his forces in an arc, with his left anchored on the Potomac River running in a northeast direction fifteen miles southeast of Frederick. McClellan was convinced that he was greatly outnumbered by the enemy and that the enemy was in motion. On September 12, McClellan received reports from Pleasonton's cavalry that the Confederates were leaving Frederick, moving in two groups toward Harper's Ferry and Hagerstown. McClellan began moving his II and IX Corps into Frederick, with troops probing beyond Frederick, in the early

Confederate soldiers traveling through Frederick, Maryland. *Library of Congress.*

morning of September 13 to maintain contact with Lee's army. To the south, Franklin's VI Corps continued to move north toward Buckeystown. Lee in the meantime had moved troops to the high ground surrounding Harper's Ferry, with Longstreet and D.H. Hill moving toward Boonsboro and Hagerstown.

This was the distribution of Lee's and McClellan's forces when a copy of Lee's Special Orders No. 191, wrapped with three cigars, was found by the 27th Indiana Infantry outside Frederick on September 13. The order was quickly delivered up the chain of command to General McClellan's headquarters. A staff office of the division of the 27th Indiana had known, before the war, Colonel R.H. Chilton, Lee's assistant adjutant general, who had written the order. Chilton's handwriting was verified, and the order was confirmed as authentic by Pleasonton's cavalry that afternoon. Long after the war, it was reported that with this information General McClellan boasted to General John Gibbon that he now knew Lee's intent and would attack and defeat the Confederates in detail. "Here I have a paper," he said, "with which if I cannot whip Bobby Lee, I will be willing to go home."[71] McClellan wired President Lincoln at midnight on the thirteenth: "I think Lee has made a gross mistake, and that he will be severely punished for it. The army is in motion as rapidly as possible."[72]

On September 11, prior to the discovery of Special Orders No. 191, McClellan reported to General Halleck that he was confronting a gigantic Rebel army[73] and requested reinforcements. General McClellan continued his habit of overestimating the size of his opponent. He estimated a Rebel force between 120,000 and 200,000 facing his 85,000 troops. The Confederate total strength probably never exceeded 55,000.[74] Special Orders No. 191 indicated movement of the command without indicating the Confederate army's strength. McClellan was left to his own estimates that had proven to be grossly overstated during the Peninsula Campaign. Since the order was four days old when discovered, immediate action was necessary to take advantage of the widespread Confederate force. For reasons unknown, General McClellan delayed fourteen hours before major movement was ordered against Lee's scattered forces. Receiving Special Orders No. 191 around noon, McClellan began issuing orders in the late afternoon for movement on September 14. None of the movement of a significant number of troops near South Mountain and the entry to Lee's army was to take place before early morning on September 14, and in none of the orders was a sense of urgency noted. This was especially true of orders to General Franklin, who had only a twelve-mile march to the summit of Crampton's Gap that could have been accomplished during the day on September 13, with little risk, or even that night with the route available to him.[75] Only General Pleasonton was expected to use his cavalry to probe Confederate forces guarding the approaches to South Mountain. General Lee, in his August 19, 1863 report on the Maryland operations, indicated that McClellan "immediately…pushed forward rapidly."[76] Often used as basis for McClellan's "rapid movement," Lee's comment related only to Pleasonton's cavalry probe. On the evening of the thirteenth, McClellan did order the advance of Burnside in preparation for an attack on South Mountain on the fourteenth and moved Hooker closer to Frederick. Important time, however, was lost in the delay of McClellan's other troops—time that would be reflected in the action at the gaps of South Mountain. Another reason for movement delays often offered was congestion at Frederick. A better part of three corps were in the Frederick area. Except for the Monocacy River, the area around Frederick could accommodate large forces without entering the town; nonetheless, the town became a bottleneck. McClellan remarked about the wonderful reception, "Men, Women and children crowded around us, weeping, shouting, and praying; they clung around old Dan's neck and almost suffocated the old fellow, decking him out with flags."[77] General McClellan was in his element.

General Lee, not knowing the fate of the copy intercepted by the Union of Special Orders No. 191, continued to manage his far-flung command, believing that McClellan would continue a slow advance toward South Mountain. General McClellan now had a blueprint for the intentions of General Lee. He had only to efficiently manage his time and command to meet and defeat General Lee and the Confederate army.

Chapter 6

SOUTH MOUNTAIN AND HARPER'S FERRY

S ome believe that South Mountain was a part of the Antietam battle. Others believe that it was a separate and distinct operation. Clearly, South Mountain was a critical prelude to the September 17, 1862 Battle of Antietam; the Union success at the gaps of South Mountain was the high point to Lee's invasion of Maryland and Pennsylvania. Had McClellan acted quicker with his cavalry under General Pleasonton investing Turner's Gap earlier, the Battle of Antietam may have been substantially different. Had General Franklin demonstrated a sense of urgency on his movement to Crampton's Gap, the results of Harper's Ferry and the entire campaign might have changed. South Mountain was a credit to both the Confederacy and the Union. General D.H. Hill delayed bravely with a small force at Turner's and Fox's Gaps against aggressive Union forces, willing to engage in hand-to-hand combat.

The morning of September 14, General D.H. Hill initially had, at most, 2,300 men, including a 200-man cavalry regiment from General Stuart, to defend Turner's Gap, the primary Union route to the west of South Mountain.[78] McClellan sent General Alfred Pleasonton's cavalry and a single brigade from General Jessie Reno's IX Corps to break through Turner's Gap. Following was General Joseph Hooker and his I Corps. Hooker had a much longer march from east of Frederick and would not arrive until the late afternoon.

At about 9:00 a.m., some 3,000 men from the Ohio brigades of Colonel Eliakim Scammon and Colonel George Crook met about 1,000 North

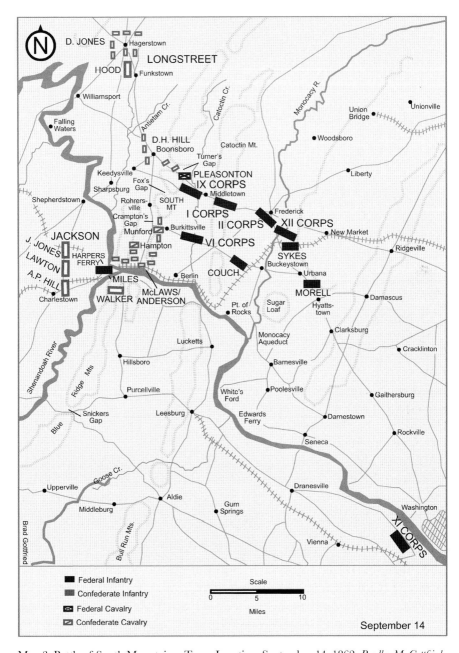

Map 3. Battle of South Mountain—Troop Location, September 14, 1862. *Bradley M. Gottfried.*

Carolina troops under General Samuel Garland, along with dismounted cavalry and one battery of artillery at Fox's Gap. Musket fire supported by artillery on both sides opened the engagement. The Union advance against the stubborn Confederates resulted in brutal hand-to-hand combat with fists, bayonets and muskets as clubs. By noon, the Confederates had been routed and had fled west, still awaiting the three remaining brigades of Hill's command arriving from Boonsboro, bringing no more than 5,000 total troops, engaged at Turner's and Fox's Gaps, based on General Hill's after-action report.[79]

With Reno's lead troops at Fox's Gap resting after the pitched fight with Hill, units of the Union army were slow in moving to support the IX Corps. Supporting units under General Joseph Hooker did not arrive to continue actions at Turner's Gap until 2:00 p.m. By this time, the remaining troops of General Hill had arrived from Boonsboro to continue the defense of the gap. General Longstreet's command had begun turning toward Turner's Gap from Hagerstown that morning. It was not expected to arrive for several hours. Upon the arrival of two brigades from Longstreet, Hill sent them south to Fox's Gap to join brigades of General George Anderson and Roswell Ripley. The I Corps under General Joseph Hooker at Turner's Gap and the remainder of General Reno's IX Corps at Fox's Gap at last prevailed. General D.H. Hill was forced to abandon Turner's Gap before daylight on September 15, 1862. The delay by General Hill at Turner's and Fox's Gaps until the morning of September 15 provided Lee with valuable time to consolidate his dispersed command.

Meanwhile, at Crampton's Gap, six miles from Turner's Gap, General McLaws, on nearby Maryland Heights, was at risk for an attack at his rear by Union General William Franklin and the VI Corps. Franklin was ordered to move to Crampton's Gap at daybreak on September 14.[80] If Franklin acted rapidly and prevailed over McLaws, Harper's Ferry might be saved. At 2:00 p.m. on September 14, the division of Major General Henry Slocum and two brigades of Major General William "Baldy" Smith met three Virginia regiments commanded by Colonel William Parham and the dismounted cavalry of Thomas Munford. General Franklin spent more than three hours assessing the situation at Crampton's Gap until 4:00 p.m., when he ordered a general advance against the Confederate forces. Initially routed, the Confederates could not delay Slocum and Smith and reformed in Pleasant Valley. General McClellan had ordered Franklin to destroy or capture McLaws's forces. Apparently, Franklin thought that succeeding at Crampton's Gap was enough to meet McClellan's order.

South Mountain from Antietam Cemetery. *Library of Congress.*

Union forces ultimately stopped any planned advance from Crampton's Gap when artillery fire on the fifteenth indicated that Harper's Ferry had surrendered.

With the questionable victory at Crampton's Gap, South Mountain was in the hands of the Union. Unfortunately, it was too late for General McClellan to engage and defeat General Lee's scattered forces. McClellan reported that the Battle of South Mountain as "a glorious victory."[81]

With the Union in control of South Mountain, placing additional pressure on the Confederates, General Lee realized that his objective of carrying the war into Pennsylvania would need to be delayed. Lee's objective now was to consolidate his troops and avoid any devastating contact with the superior numbered Union forces. Lee ordered the commands of Longstreet and D.H. Hill to retreat from Turner's Gap and McLaws from Harper's Ferry under cover of darkness and move to Sharpsburg for possible crossing of the

Potomac at Shepherdstown. At 8:00 p.m. on September 14, General Lee instructed General McLaws, "The day has gone against us and this army will go by Sharpsburg to cross the river."[82] Lee had serious concerns about the condition of his command. In a telegram to President Davis on September 13, Lee commented, "Our ranks are very much diminished—I fear a third to one half of the original numbers—though I have reason to hope that our casualties in battles will not exceed 5,000."[83]

However, reports from "Stonewall" Jackson that Harper's Ferry could be captured within days was of great interest to

Major General William Franklin. *Library of Congress.*

Lee. A victory at Harper's Ferry would allow the Confederacy to gain more than 12,000 prisoners, as well as any munitions remaining, and could save the entire invasion from total failure. The capture of Harper's Ferry also removed the Union forces that threatened Lee's logistic line and allowed Lee to renew his invasion of Pennsylvania later. As a result of this information, Lee ordered his command, less those investing Harper's Ferry, into defensive positions in front of Sharpsburg, on high ground west of Antietam Creek. The investment and capture of Harper's Ferry was outlined in Special Orders No. 191 to be Friday, September 12, 1862, after a three-day march. Jackson and his forces did not establish his position on School House Ridge opposite Bolivar Heights at Harper's Ferry until Saturday, September 13. Part of his delay was his decision to go through Williamsport rather than the shorter route through Sharpsburg. Lee may also have been optimistic, believing that the garrison at Harper's Ferry would surrender without resistance.

Meanwhile, General Jackson had developed strong positions at Harper's Ferry, with Major General McLaws on Maryland Heights, Brigadier General Walker at Loudoun Heights and Jackson's remaining forces at Bolivar Heights. Confederate gunners controlled all the high ground around Harper's Ferry. The hopeless situation was understood by Colonel Benjamin Davis, 8th New York Cavalry. Davis devised a plan to break out of Harper's Ferry with his 1,300 troopers and horses. On September 14, he presented this plan to Colonel Dixon Miles, commander at Harper's Ferry. Miles initially refused permission and later relented as long as the cavalry waited until dark and did not tell the infantry.

Harper's Ferry, Virginia. *Library of Congress.*

Colonel Davis succeeded in this escape with the help of two local guides, who took them on the little-known route used by John Brown in 1859 to enter Harper's Ferry. He bypassed Sharpsburg and moved to the road connecting Williamsport with Hagerstown. There he captured General Longstreet's forty-wagon ammunition train.

At Harper's Ferry on the morning of September 15, after a barrage of artillery, Brigadier General Julius White, commander of the 2,500-strong garrison of Martinsburg who had escaped to Harper's Ferry on September 11, met with General Jackson to surrender. General White, in accordance with military protocol, deferred command to his junior, Colonel Miles, for action in the face of the enemy. In the morning artillery attack, Colonel Miles received mortal wounds; 12,700 troops later surrendered, and 13,000 small arms, 200 wagons, 73 pieces of artillery and a large supply of other material were also captured by the Confederates.[84] Leaving General A.P. Hill's division to administer paroles to the 12,700 prisoners, General Jackson moved the remainder of his command to join General Lee at Sharpsburg beginning in the afternoon and continuing through the night, arriving at noon on the sixteenth.

Left: Major General Lafayette McLaws. *Right*: Brigadier General John Walker. *Library of Congress.*

Union General Franklin received orders from General McClellan at dawn on September 15 to control Pleasant Valley to the northeast of Harper's Ferry, engage the enemy and relieve the forces at Harper's Ferry.[85] Confederate General McLaws, with 8,000 troops, was believed to have taken up defensive positions guarding the Pleasant Valley approach to Harper's Ferry. At 9:00 a.m., Franklin delayed his march, and near 11:00 a.m., he realized that Harper's Ferry had fallen and abandoned the movement forward. General McLaws continued to block access to Harper's Ferry before departing for Sharpsburg.

The surrender of the garrison at Harper's Ferry occurred three days after the date planned by Lee. This delay was critical, providing McClellan additional time to get his forces to South Mountain. Had the garrison at Harper's Ferry surrendered as anticipated, on September 12, Lee and his command would have begun movement into Pennsylvania well ahead of McClellan. This delay was a result of an overly optimistic time schedule by General Lee rather than the actions of General McClellan.

General McClellan received information that the Confederates had abandoned South Mountain during the night of September 14–15; however, he waited until 8:00 a.m. to issue orders to pursue the enemy. The lack of early and specific orders resulted in McClellan's troops being stretched for miles in pursuit of Lee. Continued caution by McClellan provided Lee an opportunity to mass his troops at Sharpsburg by September 16.

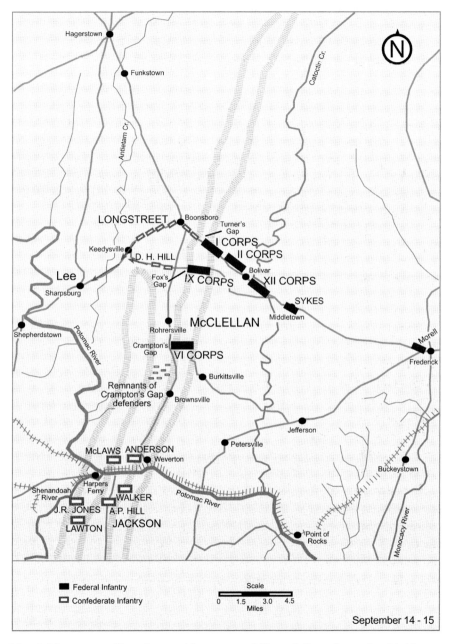

Map 4. Movement to Sharpsburg and Investment of Harper's Ferry, September 14–15, 1862. *Bradley M. Gottfried.*

Sharpsburg. *Library of Congress.*

The selection of Confederate positions at Sharpsburg has been a subject of debate by historians. Locations such as Hauser's Ridge, Reed Ridge, Sharpsburg Ridge and Harper's Ferry Road Ridge offered defensive positions. While Lee's primary position was on Sharpsburg Ridge, with artillery on Hauser's and Reed Ridge and his right on Harper's Ferry Road Ridge, some contend that these locations were selected with insufficient reconnaissance. Some also believe that General Lee's inability to conduct personal reconnaissance, as was his preference, contributed to an inferior defensive position. Just prior to departing for Maryland, Lee had suffered an accident that resulted in broken bones in one hand and the other hand severely sprained. As a result, he was unable to mount or ride a horse and was relegated to an ambulance much of the time during Antietam. While he was reported on his horse when meeting Longstreet in Boonsboro, the reins were held by a steward. This physical limitation may have affected Lee's management of the battle.

General McClellan had remained in his headquarters east of South Mountain, managing his army through dispatches. General Hooker, upon marching through Turner's Gap, reported a retreating, demoralized Army of Northern Virginia. With this information, McClellan reported exaggerated success to General Halleck in Washington that Lee was heading for Shepherdstown in a panic.[86] As expected, President Lincoln wired his thanks and congratulations for the victory.

Shortly before 1:00 p.m. on September 15, a Union observation post reported Confederate troops, probably in defensive positions, at Sharpsburg.[87] With this information, General McClellan moved to the front. It was not until 3:00 p.m. that McClellan and his staff began to assess

Lutheran Church, Sharpsburg.
Library of Congress.

the position of the enemy. They found Lee in well-chosen positions on the high ground in front of Sharpsburg with well-placed artillery. If McClellan could dislodge Lee from these positions, Lee would have only the ford over the Potomac River at Shepherdstown as an escape route. Unfortunately, while this opportunity was inviting, McClellan placed the strength of the Rebels, after an estimated 5,000 casualties at South Mountain, at 100,000 versus his 87,000 troops.[88] This manpower disadvantage to McClellan caused him to pause. Now it was too late to initiate an attack. The day available to move the eight miles from Turner's Gap to Sharpsburg to press a tired and beaten Confederate army was lost.

General Lee had placed his army in defensive positions on the high ground west of Antietam Creek in front of Sharpsburg. Roads leading through Sharpsburg offered excellent lines of communication, which were to be used effectively by Lee during the battle to move troops in support of the action. Major General Richard Anderson's and General McLaws's Divisions of Longstreet's wing were in reserve west of the town. Stuart's cavalry was to the rear of Jackson's wing, with his horse artillery facing Hagerstown Turnpike on Nicodemus Hill in front of and north of Jackson. Establishing defensive positions against a superior force with the army's back to the Potomac River, and with only Boteler's Ford at Shepherdstown available for a retreat, was unusual even with terrain assisting in restricting Union movement. It is possible that Lee believed that this strong defensive position would allow him to prevail just as the Union had succeeded at Malvern Hill during the Peninsula Campaign.

McClellan continued his reconnaissance in the early morning at an observation point on Boonsboro Turnpike about a half mile north of the center of his position and just out of range of Confederate artillery. A heavy mist impeded his work and delayed his review of enemy and friendly positions. By the time the mist had lifted and McClellan made some minor adjustments to his forces, it was 2:00 p.m. General McClellan's attack plan, now complete, would have to wait until tomorrow.

Some historians believe that on September 16, McClellan had no intention or plan to attack Lee. Rather, in keeping with his objective of forcing Lee into Virginia, his plan was to present a show of force that would result in Lee retreating across the Potomac River into Virginia. They believe that McClellan's plan for the battle on September 17 was developed the morning of the attack. This justifies McClellan's delay in his attack and the implementation of a questionable echelon attack on September 17. However, his written order to General Franklin, issued on September 15 at 1:00 a.m. to move from Pleasant Valley to Boonsboro, indicated that "the commanding general intends to attack to-morrow."[89] This would suggest that McClellan had indeed intended to attack on September 16, but the main attack was delayed until the next day.

The additional time allowed General Lee to improve his troop positioning. Beginning with about 18,000 to face McClellan, the number was increased to 36,000 with the arrival of the troops from Harper's Ferry. Lee also hoped that A.P. Hill could complete the parole of Union captives at Harper's Ferry and join the main body for the impending battle.

General McClellan began to position his army to initiate an attack in the early morning of September 17, 1862. On the afternoon of September 15, he took no action. On the morning of September 16, he had 101,100 soldiers under his command, with 75,000 at Antietam and 12,300 of Franklin's command at Pleasant Valley. Humphrey's Division of the V Corps numbered 6,600 at Frederick. Lee, with his united command, numbered under 40,000 men.[90] McClellan took no action. Now he was preparing to attack a better-organized foe. Having organized his army into three wings under Generals Burnside, Sumner and Franklin at the beginning of the campaign, McClellan now returned to his original corps organization. The Army of the Potomac was now organized into the I Corps (General Joseph Hooker), II Corps (General Edwin Sumner), V Corps (General Fitz John Porter), VI Corps (General William Franklin), IX Corps (General Ambrose Burnside, in command of his old corps after the death of General Reno) and XII Corps (Major General Joseph Mansfield).

General McClellan had squandered the advantage presented by the Lost Orders—he no longer could attack the separated Confederates and defeat

Left: Major General Joseph Hooker. *Right*: Major General Edwin Sumner. *Library of Congress.*

them in detail. General Lee was forced to either leave Maryland or face a battle at a place and time that he had not intended.

On the afternoon of September 16, McClellan and his staff made a rapid two-mile ride to observe the battlefield, drawing artillery fire from Lee. Finally, at 4:00 p.m., General Hooker began crossing Antietam Creek to take his position on the Union right flank north of the Poffenberger Farm along the Hagerstown Turnpike. He arrived at his position that evening with orders to begin the attack early the next morning, with virtually no time for reconnaissance. Burnside took up positions on the Union left flank above the Rohrbach Bridge, which would be his objective in the morning. Porter and Pleasonton's cavalry moved to positions in the center along the Boonsboro Road.

Mansfield arrived after dark and was in position the morning of September 17. General Sumner arrived by midday on the seventeenth. General Franklin, reportedly, began his march from Pleasant Valley early on the seventeenth.

The most significant tactical moves by General McClellan during the Battle of Antietam was positioning Hooker along the Hagerstown Turnpike.

Left: Major General Fitz John Porter. *Right*: Major General Joseph Mansfield. *Library of Congress.*

By reaching this location before Lee could move, Lee's preferred path north to Pennsylvania was blocked. On September 16, McClellan realized that Lee had not responded to Hooker's control of the Hagerstown Turnpike, nor was he retreating. Lee appeared to be preparing to defend against a general attack.

General McClellan's ultimate plan, accepted by many historians, was simple: attack Lee's left with Hooker while Burnside demonstrated on Lee's right to prohibit Lee from moving troops in support of "Stonewall" Jackson on his left. McClellan's reserves, in the center, would then attack either Lee's left or center to destroy the Army of Northern Virginia. It is interesting to note that McClellan, in his autobiography, *McClellan's Own Story*, stated that Burnside's action was to take place after Hooker successfully turned Lee's left flank.[91] McClellan's plan, which included a diversionary attack by Burnside, was outlined only in his after-action report dated October 15.[92] Some modern historians theorize that McClellan's plan for the morning of September 17 was developed that morning, after

Lee failed to retreat.[93] It is difficult to determine the basis for the attack, since no written orders were provided to McClellan's corps commanders. Evidence of his plan was contained in his after-action report, written four weeks after the battle.

McClellan's simple plan had merit but was dependent on good communications, adequate reconnaissance of the route of attack and timely orders. As was customary during the war, army commander McClellan remained at his headquarters, well back from the points of attack. During this time, McClellan appeared to have little contact with his subordinates. His orders to corps commanders were inadequately simple and allowed little time for his commanders to plan their attack. Without clear instructions to his commanders, McClellan's initial attack on Lee's left soon became chaotic. Corps commanders went to the front of their attack, thus losing control of their men. Units were committed in an uncoordinated fashion, and commanders on the Union right were on their own. Similarly, Lee's commands were brief and general without written support. This contributed to the chaotic situation.

The primary flaw in General McClellan's plan was that it totally discounted his advantage of numbers. During the battle, the Union enjoyed a better than two-to-one advantage over the Rebels. McClellan supporters argue that the number of troops engaged is open to question. Accepting their arguments, McClellan's advantage was, at least, one and a half to one. Attacking in echelon, without Burnside's demonstration, allowed Lee to move troops to the point of attack, leaving their former positions substantially unprotected. As General Sumner commented, "Sending those troops into action in driblets, as they were sent" was the cause of the bloody Wednesday.[94] Had McClellan used a broad attack against the whole of the Confederate front, it is thought that a major victory could have been achieved, annihilating the Rebel force.

As the battle opened, General Hooker was located on the right near the Hagerstown Turnpike. The XII Corps of General Mansfield was in the center to the left of Hooker and farther north. Sumner's Corps was in the center, east of Antietam Creek; General Burnside was on the left near Rohrbach Bridge, the most southerly of the three bridges spanning the creek. General Porter was in reserve in the center, along with Pleasonton's cavalry. The third division of Sumner's Corps, commanded by General William French, provided security to McClellan's headquarters, located east of Antietam Creek at the home of Philip Pry, about two miles from General Hooker's right flank, in the center of the Union line. General Franklin began his march toward the battle from his position at Pleasant Valley near Crampton's Gap in South Mountain.

In Washington, D.C., McClellan's announcements were received with skepticism. They had heard McClellan's boasts of success dashed by reality in the past. Lincoln was pleased by reports of the pursuit of Lee but discouraged by reports of the loss of Harper's Ferry. Conditions in the west had deteriorated, as identified by General Halleck in mid-June.[95] In Kentucky, Confederates controlled the capital of Frankfort, and General Braxton Bragg was pressuring 4,000 Union forces at Munfordville. Cincinnati was preparing defenses for the city. Meanwhile, England watched progress of the war closely.

As Washington and the world watched, General Lee and General McClellan began a deadly chess game that would have major impact on the war.

Chapter 7

THE BATTLE OF ANTIETAM

S eptember 17, 1862, would be the bloodiest day in the history of this country. No single day since has produced more casualties: 22,719 men killed, wounded or missing. The Union had 12,401 casualties, representing nearly 25 percent of those who went into battle; 2,108 were killed.[96] The Confederate army suffered 10,310, or 31 percent, casualties of those who entered the battle; 1,546 were killed.[97] Total casualties in the Maryland Campaign were approximately 41,000—14,000 Confederates and 27,000 Union, including 11,500 captured at Harper's Ferry.[98] The 1st Texas Regiment of Hood's Division suffered the greatest casualty rate, 82.3 percent, of any regiment in the Civil War; 226 men were present at Antietam, 45 killed and 141 wounded.[99]

At dawn on September 17, General Hooker initiated the attack on the right of the Union line, beginning about one mile from his objective: a plateau east of the Hagerstown Turnpike where the whitewashed Dunker Church was located. A breakthrough of this heavily defended area could be a mortal blow to the Army of Northern Virginia. The Confederate batteries of Stuart's horse artillery on Nicodemus Hill, west of the Hagerstown Turnpike, opened the battle at dawn by dueling with the Union artillery of General Abner Doubleday.

Hooker's I Corps attacked from the North Woods in front of Joseph Poffenberger's farm, with Brigadier General Doubleday's division on the right, attacking along and on both sides of the Hagerstown Turnpike. Brigadier General George Meade and his 3rd Division, in the center, would

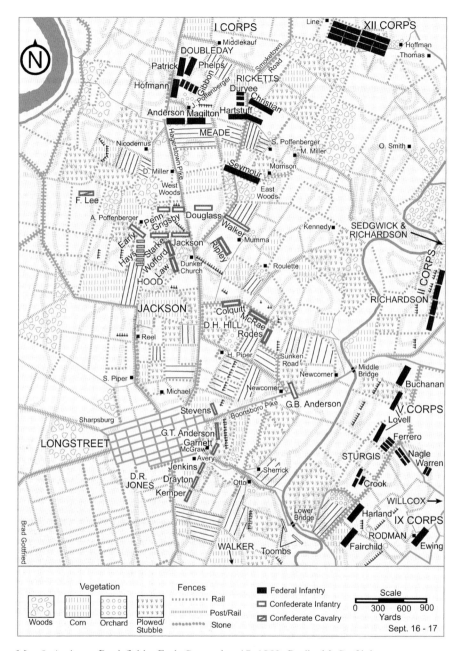

Map 5. Antietam Battlefield—Early September 17, 1862. *Bradley M. Gottfried.*

The dead along Hagerstown Turnpike. *Library of Congress Library of Congress.*

Row of dead awaiting burial after the Battle of Antietam. *Library of Congress.*

back up Doubleday. Brigadier General James Rickett was on the left, attacking through the East Woods. Hooker's 8,600 Union soldiers would meet in the twenty four-acre cornfield of David R. Miller, slightly less than halfway to the Dunker Church. This field will forever be remembered simply as "the Cornfield."

General McClellan provided little direction to Hooker. As a result, Hooker began the offensive on his own schedule. McClellan's plan for the battle, reported by historians, included early pressure on the right by Burnside. McClellan, in his autobiography, indicated that Burnside would begin his movement "as matters looked favorable."[100] This raises the question whether Burnside was to advance concurrently with Hooker's attack. A delay in the attack by Burnside gave Lee the opportunity to move troops to his right from his left to meet the Union advances. The ability of Lee to shift troops along this north/south line of communications was critical to his overpowered command being able to maximize the limited troops available to him.

Between 6:00 a.m. and 7:30 a.m. that morning, Hooker's divisions fought "Stonewall" Jackson's wing from the North and East Woods through the cornfield, which was head high and fully mature. Hood's counterattack, at about 7:00 a.m., forced the Union troops back and forth through the cornfield. This exchange through the cornfield was the first of many. Rickett's Division was driven back in full retreat, losing one-third as casualties. Brigadier General John R. Jones of Jackson's wing led his division as the primary defenders on Lee's left, about a quarter of a mile north of the Dunker Church in the West Woods. General Alexander Lawton had his division east of the Hagerstown Turnpike north of the Dunker Church. Jackson could provide about 7,700 troops on this flank. Jackson's forces began a fierce counterattack from the West Woods that drove Hooker's Union forces out of the cornfield to Miller's barnyard, where Union artillery, firing double canister, slowed Jackson's advance. Lee, realizing that additional forces would be needed, called for General Longstreet to detach General John Hood's 2,300-man division from Lee's right to the West Woods, just west of the church. The remainder of Longstreet's wing remained on Lee's right, stretched toward Snavely's Ford, where a detachment of Stuart's cavalry screened the flank. Divisions of General Robert Anderson and General Lafayette McLaws provided Longstreet's reserve west of the town of Sharpsburg.

General Hooker called for support of the XII Corps, commanded by General Joseph Mansfield, which was east of the East Woods. At the same time, Hooker committed the last of his reserve troops under Brigadier General Meade. Despite Hooker's advances of more than an hour, McClellan's

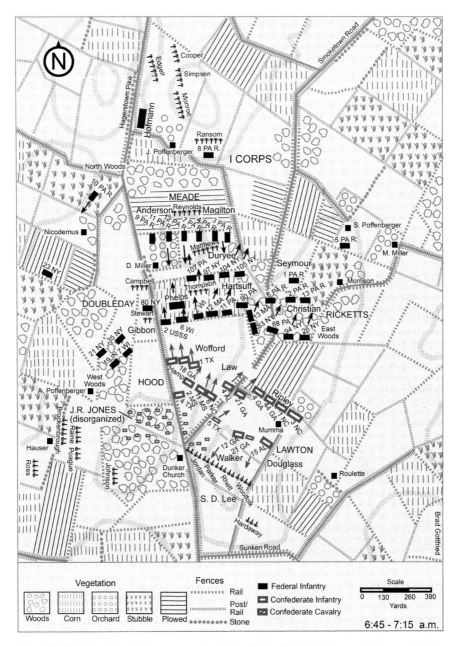

Map 6. Initial Attack and Counterattack—Union Right Flank, 5:15 a.m.–7:45 a.m. *Bradley M. Gottfried.*

Brigadier General John B. Hood.
Library of Congress.

promise of other attacks to be conducted concurrently did not materialize. As the battle continued, the cornfield was the site of some of the bloodiest struggles of the entire war. Musket and canister fire from artillery punctuated the battle, with the cornfield constantly changing hands. Commanders on horseback rode carefully so as not to tread on the dead and wounded. General Hooker noted in his official report of the battle on November 8, 1862, "In the time I am writing, every stalk of corn in the northern and greater part of the field was cut as closely as with a knife and the slain lay in rows precisely as they stood in their ranks a few minutes before. It was never my fortune to witness a more bloody, dismal battlefield."[101]

By 7:30 a.m., Hooker had nearly one-third casualties of those engaged; Rickett's losses were the greatest of the corps. None of Hooker's divisions could renew the attack once General Mansfield and his 7,200 troops arrived on the field. General Joseph Mansfield was a senior corps commander, with more than forty years of military experience, who had only taken command on September 15. The presence of Mansfield's Corps marching into battle in close formation caused Jackson's men in the cornfield to retreat to the West Woods. Part of Hood's command had entered the East Woods while there were still Union units in the cornfield. General Mansfield was hit and mortally wounded near the East Woods. Brigadier General Alpheus Williams took command and renewed the battle for the cornfield.

Between 7:00 a.m. and 9:00 a.m., the renewal of the battle on the Union right was in the hands of the Union XII Corps and D.H. Hill's division of General Jackson's wing. D.H. Hill had been positioned near the Sunken Road, south of the initial battle. He moved his units north through the Mumma Farm to engage the Union forces, while the remnants of Hood's forces held on to the West Woods. Brigadier General Alfred Colquitt's brigade of D.H. Hill's division engaged Union infantry in the trampled cornfield and were turned back by withering fire.

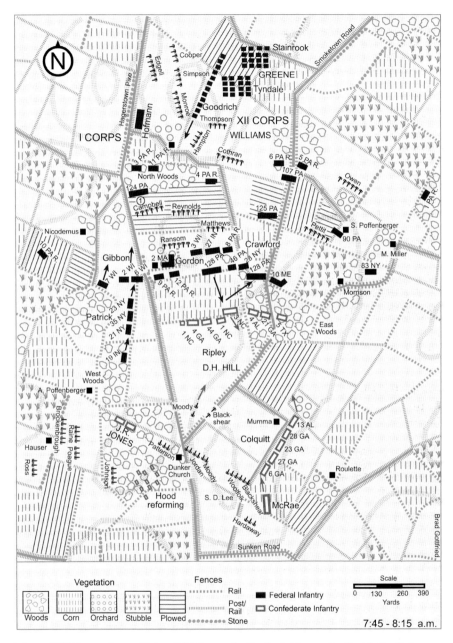

Map 7. XII Corps, General Mansfield Enters the Battle, 7:45 a.m. *Bradley M. Gottfried.*

Left: Brigadier General George Meade. *Right*: Brigadier General Alpheus Williams. *Library of Congress.*

By 9:00 a.m., General Hooker had been wounded and removed from the field. General Jackson was consolidating his thinned ranks to defend the Confederate left flank awaiting reinforcements. In just the first three hours of the engagement on the Union right and Confederate left, more than 8,000 men were killed or wounded. At this time, General Sedgewick's division of Sumner's Corps arrived and engaged with the XII Corps in support.[102]

General Edwin Sumner and his II Corps were located south and east of the initial engagement by Generals Hooker and Mansfield. Sumner was sixty-five years old, the oldest of the Union corps commanders. McClellan had reservations about Sumner's ability to command a unit the size of a corps and kept him on a short leash. Sumner was prepared to support action on the morning of September 17; however, he was ordered to remain in position on the east side of Antietam Creek and await orders by General McClellan. Orders were yet to be received as the fighting continued to 9:00 a.m. General McClellan remained at Pry's house during much of the morning. He had restricted views of Hooker and Mansfield, as well as Burnside on his left. Most of his information on the battle came from flag signals from the Union observation post on Elk Mountain about four miles to the south.[103] As a result of his incomplete information on the

Confederate dead near the Dunker Church. *Library of Congress.*

Dead at the fence line along the Hagerstown Turnpike. *Library of Congress.*

status of the battle, he was reluctant to engage the II Corps and its 15,800 infantry troops.

At about 9:00 a.m., Sumner was ready to support the Union attack on the right or north of the field. Most of Hooker's troops were spent and had moved north to their original position at Poffenberger's farm. Williams's XII Corps was spread throughout the battlefield attempting to hold the positions the men had gained that morning. The battle on the Union right became a free-for-all.

On the Union left, by 8:00 a.m., General Burnside was alerted by McClellan to open his IX Corps attack on Rohrbach Bridge, the farthest south of the three bridges on the battlefield crossing the sluggish Antietam Creek. This bridge, after this date, would forever be known as Burnside Bridge.

The attack by Burnside was critical to the Union plan to place pressure on the Confederate right, prohibiting Lee from moving troops to support General Jackson and the left of the Confederate line. Finally, at 9:00 a.m., McClellan determined that it was safe to direct the attack by the IX Corps. McClellan's delay in ordering Burnside to attack appeared to be his early commitment of Sumner's Corps and his desire to determine the outcome of Hooker, Mansfield and Sumner on his right.[104] He also notified General Franklin, whose VI Corps was approaching from Pleasant Valley, to provide two divisions to supplement the army reserve. General Burnside received McClellan's order about 10:00 a.m., too late to challenge the right flank of Lee and relieve the pressure on the Union forces fighting on the right and center of the Union line.

About this time, Brigadier General William French's division of Sumner's II Corps, in cooperation with Major General Israel Richardson's division, shifted its attack to the left of General George Greene of the XII Corps, which was holding raised ground in front of the Dunker Church. French's shift to the center and the Sunken Road rather than supporting Greene at the West Woods appeared to be without orders and changed the dynamics of the Union right. With this change in the battle, McClellan realized that he must weaken the center and ordered two of Franklin's divisions arriving from Pleasant Valley to support the Union right.[105] The remainder of the XII Corps had been repulsed at the West Woods at the Hagerstown Turnpike.

In the meantime, on the Union right, General John Sedgewick's division of the II Corps was being pursued by McLaws's Division of Longstreet's wing, which had joined Jackson in the action on Lee's left. Sedgewick was forced north toward Miller's farm after suffering tremendous casualties.

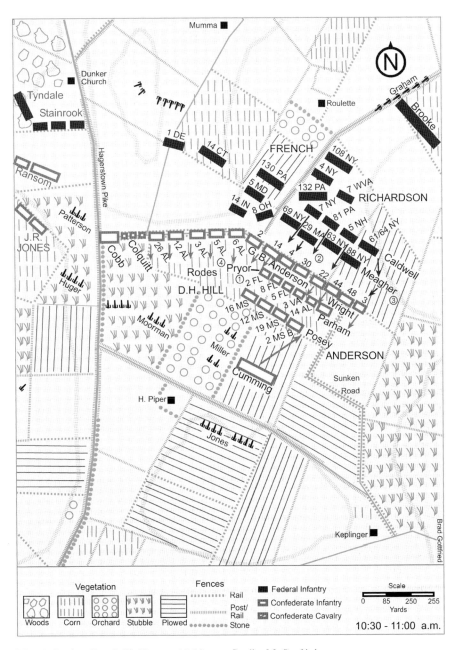

Map 8. Sunken Road, 10:30 a.m.–11:00 a.m. *Bradley M. Gottfried.*

As action on the Union right slowed after repeated attacks and withdrawals, the battle now shifted to the Confederate center. General D.H. Hill of Jackson's wing was in the center, about five hundred yards south of the Dunker Church, in a strong defensive position along a farm road that ran east and south from the Hagerstown Turnpike. The Sunken Road would hereafter be known as the Bloody Lane. Union General French attacked General Hill across the fields of the Mumma Farm and the orchard and pasture of the Roulette Farm. The route of the march was across slightly rising terrain, resulting in a low ridge in front of the Sunken Road. Except for this terrain feature, the landscape offered no cover for the attacking Union forces. The initial attack was greeted by a strong volley of Confederate fire, less than one hundred yards from the Union attackers, immediately causing French's men to retreat behind the ridge to lay down to return fire. Colonel Dwight Morris and the 2nd Brigade followed the initial attack. These unseasoned troops were met by the same effective fire as the initial advance and were also driven back. General Longstreet ordered a counterattack on the left side of the line. Confederate troops led by Brigadier General Robert Rodes were repelled with the same result that awaited the Union forces attacking the Sunken Road. Rodes was forced to withdraw back to the Bloody Lane. The third Union attempt to take the Sunken Road was attempted by Brigadier General Nathan Kimball's brigade of French's Division. The veteran soldiers in that brigade dropped back behind the low ridge in front of the sunken road and crawled back to the top to fire. The Union line stabilized and began to look for the Confederate flank. While General French's men were spent, they continued to fight and hold their position opposite the Sunken Road.

At 10:30 a.m., the conflict at the Sunken Road continued, as the situation to the right at the Dunker Church and beyond began to stabilize. At this point, 4,000 men of Union General Israel Richardson's command arrived from Antietam Creek to support French. General Richard Anderson's troops, initially reserves for General Longstreet, moved up to supplement Hill's command. The battle at the Sunken Road was an infantry engagement. Artillery on both sides was reluctant to fire in that direction for fear of hitting friendly soldiers. Artillery fire was

Brigadier General Robert Rodes.
Library of Congress.

concentrated on the area immediately behind the line. General Anderson was wounded by artillery fire south of the Sunken Road before he could deliver his troops to General Hill. Beyond the Union line, Confederate artillery struck beehives on Roulette's farm, angering a large swarm of bees, causing yet another challenge to Union forces. General Richardson now began his attack to the left of French's men. As his men approached the Bloody Lane, they received the same reception as had previous assaults. Like French, Richardson's men sought refuge behind the ridge facing the Sunken Road. Brigadier General John Caldwell, who assumed command from the wounded General Richardson after he was struck near the end of the fight for the road, slowly maneuvered his unit to the far right of Hill's troops in the Sunken Road. Placing the Confederates in the Sunken Road to enfilade fire, Caldwell's troops delivered deadly fire down the Sunken Road. This situation and a small salient left by Rodes's retreat from the Sunken Road subjected the left of Hill's position to withering fire from the Union. At this point in the battle in the Sunken Road, Lee had committed the last of his reserves. The Union failed to take advantage or the gain in the center largely as a result of effective Confederate artillery fire. McClellan did not provide any reinforcements from troops immediately available (Porter's V Corps). Franklin, who had arrived from Pleasant Valley, was eager to attack, but McClellan, after consulting with Sumner, withheld his approval beyond a brigade-level attack. The rest of the VI Corps held the line of the exhausted I, II and XII Corps. With a little effort, the center of the Confederate line may have collapsed, leaving the left of Lee in the air.

To relieve pressure on General Hill, Longstreet ordered Colonel John Cooke of McLaws's Division and 1,000 men to attack Brigadier General George Greene on the plain in front of the Dunker Church. Green believed that Sedgewick was to his right in the West Woods. As soon as Cooke attacked, and with information from a staff officer of Sumner's Corps, Greene realized that he was alone on the field. Shortly after the initial attack, Greene's command fell back to the rising ground to the east of the Dunker Church. Cooke and his small command, now numbering about 675 men, turned to attack the right flank of the Union at the Sunken Road. After initially threating the Union forces, counterattacks by Union forces of General French and a shortness of ammunition by Cooke's forces resulted in Cooke retiring. General Hill's and General Anderson's men were forced from the Bloody Lane to the Piper Farm. The battle for the Sunken Road had lasted for more than three hours, and General Hill still clung to the hope of defeating the Union forces facing him.

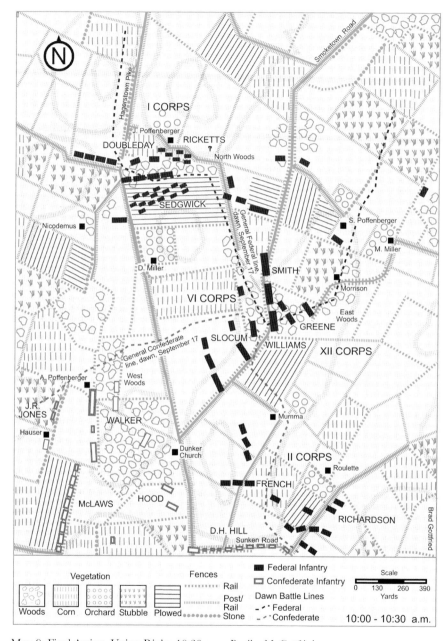

Map 9. Final Action, Union Right, 10:30 a.m. *Bradley M. Gottfried.*

The dead at the Bloody Lane. *Library of Congress.*

Nearly 2,600 men, or 30 percent of the Confederate forces at the Sunken Road, were killed. On the remainder of the Confederate lines, there was a shortage of officers to manage the Confederate forces that were mixed from a variety of units. Many units reported being out of ammunition. Just before 1:00 p.m., General Richardson withdrew his forces beyond the Sunken Road to the protection of the ridge. As Richardson planned to resume the attack on Hill, he received a mortal wound from Confederate fire. With General Hooker's corps, now under command of General George Meade, forced back to its starting point at Poffenberger's farm, and the XII Corps disorganized throughout the battlefield, the battle on the right and center of the Union was spent.

During this lull, General McClellan reported to Washington his optimistic assessment of the battle. This report was provided despite the failed attempt to turn to flank Lee and at the cost of two corps commanders wounded, one mortally. McClellan's remaining corps engaged had yet to make any progress at the Burnside Bridge; one corps and his cavalry were, along with Sykes's Division of the V Corps, engaged in the center, and one corps provided only a few units to the engagement. The 1st Division of the IV Corps, commanded by Major General Darius Couch, assigned to

Left: Major General Ambrose Burnside. *Right*: Brigadier General Jacob Cox. *Library of Congress.*

Franklin's VI Corps, spent September 17 near Harper's Ferry and did not arrive at Antietam until late that evening. General Burnside was to begin his assault on the Rohrbach or Lower Bridge at 10:00 a.m., after receiving warning orders from McClellan earlier in the morning. General McClellan had restructured his command, placing Hooker's I Corps to the right of the Union and the IX Corps, commanded by Cox, to the left. This left Burnside temporarily without a command.[106] As Cox was the senior officer on the left, orders from McClellan were routed through Burnside, who then communicated them to Cox. This confusing and complex structure led to poor communications. From the time of the early-warning orders to attack on the left, neither Burnside nor Cox conducted, or caused to be conducted, any reconnaissance of their area of responsibility. As a result, both were unaware of the conditions of Antietam Creek, which was fordable just south of the bridge.

By the time McClellan determined that it was safe for Burnside to begin the attack on Rohrbach Bridge, the value of this move was diminished. Lee had been able to move troops from his right to the center and left of the battlefield in support of action in those sectors. Burnside and Cox, in the meantime, began their attack. About 3,000 men, roughly one quarter

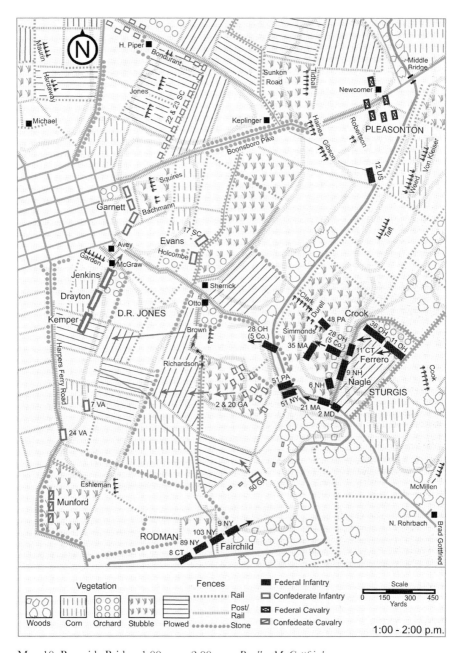

Map 10. Burnside Bridge, 1:00 p.m.–2:00 p.m. *Bradley M. Gottfried.*

of the corps under command of Brigadier General Isaac Rodman, were sent south to cross Antietam Creek downstream at a ford selected by McClellan's engineers. The first attempt to approach the bridge was easily repelled by Georgia infantrymen and artillery in strong positions on high ground west of the bridge. The initial attacking units got lost on their way along Rohrbach Bridge Road to the bridge. In the meantime, Rodman discovered that the ford site selected by the engineers was not usable because the banks of the creek were too steep for the horses. With the help of a local farmer, Rodman found a suitable crossing at Snavely's Ford farther downstream. This ford had not been located by the Union—a job normally assigned to the inert cavalry. The new ford extended the march of two-thirds of a mile to more than two miles.

The next attempt to storm the bridge, also along Rohrbach Bridge Road, was met by strong fire that pinned the attackers 250 yards from the bridge. The final attempt to cross did not take place until after noon. The 51st New York and 51st Pennsylvania, under the command of Brigadier General Edward Ferrero of Brigadier General Samuel Sturgis's division, attacked the bridge over 300 yards of open ground directly downhill to the bridge. Finally, at 1:00 p.m., after a long firefight, Burnside had his bridge.

The Burnside/Cox command was now expected to join Rodman's Division and threaten the right flank of Lee's line. McClelland failed to deliver on his promise to support Burnside with units of Fitz John Porter's V Corps, except for Warren's Brigade from Sykes's Division and Miller's Battery, and delays in resupply of ammunition to the IX Corps slowed Burnside's movement. It was not until after 2:00 p.m. that the last of Burnside's troops reached the bridge. Some of the delay was the delinquent arrival of ammunition and other logistic support. Further, Burnside had to get his corps through the bottleneck of the twelve-foot-wide bridge—9,000 infantry, 22 cannons and 132 horses choked the narrow space.[107] Slowly, around 3:00 p.m., Burnside's men moved forward toward Sharpsburg. The IX Corps continued to press the Confederates from ridge to ridge toward Sharpsburg. At this time, most of the action on the Union right and center had nearly stopped. Burnside's current operation was the only opportunity to destroy Lee's army. Had the support of Porter's command been provided, it is possible, with Burnside's IX Corps, that Lee's right flank could have been rolled up. About 3:30 p.m., A.P. Hill and his division arrived on the battlefield after a grueling seventeen-mile forced march in nine hours from Harper's Ferry.[108] Hill's slightly more than 3,000 troops, who completed the march, provided the

Burnside Bridge. *Library of Congress.*

necessary number to shore up Lee's right. Ultimately, by 5:30 p.m., Burnside was forced to retire to the first ridge line on the west side of Antietam Creek.

Action on the right and center of the Union line had continued to slow to periodic skirmishes. McClellan's reaction was to do little to take advantage of any opportunities. He continued to hold Porter's Corps in reserve and refused continued use of his cavalry for any purpose other than rounding up stragglers. At this point, nearly 20,000 men had not been committed, nearly one quarter of his army. About 10,000 troops from Franklin's VI Corps had arrived on the battlefield by 11:00 a.m. and were available for engagement. However, McClellan decided, "It would not be prudent to make the advance."[109]

The battle had run its course, and both sides settled into recovery and resupply from the bloody day. Lee's army was badly damaged, with nearly all his troops committed.[110] McClellan, on the other hand, had committed only about 56,000, with one quarter of his command not involved in the fight.[111] Yet McClellan believed that his command could not continue the attack due to losses during September 17. It is estimated that on September

18, McClellan had available nearly 20,000 men from those engaged during the day and more than 20,000 present for duty in the units not committed. The number of uncommitted troops available to McClellan has been in dispute—those who argue that the number available was substantially less than 20,000 base their estimates on the number of troops "engaged." Strength reports indicate 55,956 engaged for McClellan. This number, however, fails to account for any availability of the 87,164 troop strength reported or 31,208 men not engaged. The I, II, IV and XII Corps, which were actively engaged at Antietam on September 17, averaged 77 percent of roster strength engaged. If 77 percent is applied to Porter's V Corps, 6,732 were available, 6,885 would be available from Franklin's VI Corps and 4,320 from Pleasonton's Cavalry. This would provide a total of 17,937 uncommitted troops. Suffice it to say, there were considerable Union forces not engaged at Antietam.[112] Another reason for not committing available forces was the fact that they were new and untried. Only at Antietam is this untrained excuse used for not engaging available troops in a major battle.

With the arrival of Brigadier General Andrew Humphreys and his 3rd Division of Porter's V Corps that evening from Frederick, an additional 6,600 men were available. By the morning of the eighteenth, McClellan had nearly 50,000 men available for action. Lee had about 20,000 infantry and artillery, plus 4,500 cavalry manning his defensive position. Yet McClellan failed to order an attack on September 18. McClellan was unable to identify any weak points in Lee's new position. Much of this was a result of Lee's utilization of terrain rather than faulty planning by McClellan.[113] McClellan had accomplished the second of his three objectives—he had blocked Lee from invading Pennsylvania—and it was likely that Lee would be driven from Maryland, accomplishing his final objective.

While McClellan consolidated his forces, Lee established more effective defensive positions at Sharpsburg, now oriented with the front facing southeast, in anticipation of additional action the next day. There were no meaningful demonstrations by either side on September 18. Both sides exchanged wounded and went about the grim task of burying their dead. The Battle of Antietam was over. September 17, 1862, has the distinction of being the bloodiest day in U.S. history. Casualties of Lee's army were between 10,000 and 14,000 (1,546 dead), compared to 12,400 total Union casualties (2,108 dead). As significant, in terms of the war, was the fact that McClellan had not smashed Lee's army, in spite of having nearly twice the men available to fight. The cavalry of Pleasonton was massed in the center by McClellan, providing little support to the Union flanks.

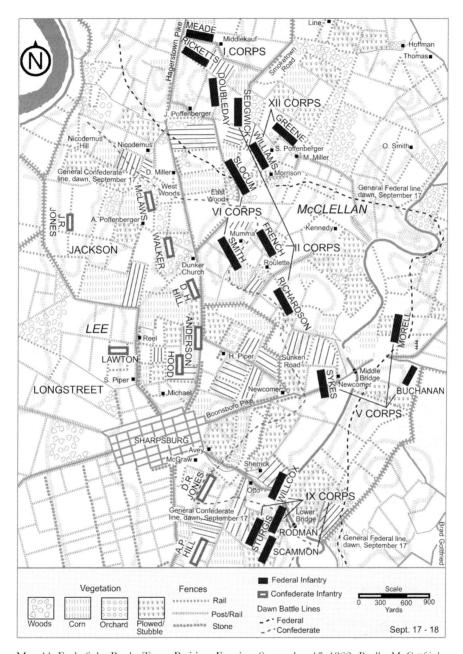

Map 11. End of the Battle, Troop Position, Evening, September 17, 1862. *Bradley M. Gottfried.*

McClellan failed to engage six of seventeen divisions. Two, commanded by Couch and Humphreys, arrived on the battlefield too late; an additional two, commanded by Smith and Slocum, arrived midday and were available only in support; and finally, divisions commanded by Morell and Sykes, after an engagement in the center, remained in reserve. Never again during the Civil War was there such an opportunity to crush the Confederate army. On September 17, McClellan did not consult any of his commanders except Fitz John Porter. The capabilities of the Army of the Northern Virginia to continue to operate after the battle were largely unknown to General McClellan. He appeared to be satisfied that his army had blunted Lee's invasion into the North and believed that the Confederate army would soon retreat into Virginia.

On the night of September 18, 1862, Lee began to move his command of about 30,000 men[114] to cross the Potomac at Boteler's Ford, just below Shepherdstown, moving to Martinsburg, leaving a small contingent of infantry to protect their withdrawal. General Porter crossed the Potomac but was driven back by A.P. Hill's counterattack on September 20. The deadliest one-day battle in the history of the country was over. Lee was driven back into Virginia, and Maryland and Pennsylvania were safe. McClellan's three objectives had been met. He protected Washington and Baltimore, he prohibited Lee from reaching Pennsylvania and he drove Lee back into Virginia.[115] This, reported by General McClellan to General Halleck, marked the beginning of the end of McClelland's command and began the trials of Lincoln finding a general who could destroy General Lee. On September 19, Stuart eased the river crossing at Williamsport, within striking distance of Pennsylvania. McClellan reacted with unusual rapid action and sent two brigades of Pleasonton's cavalry to Williamsport, followed by three divisions of infantry. Stuart realized that he was over matched and withdrew. Lee remained silent when communicating with President Davis as to why he had abandoned his second attempt to move north.

On September 19, with soldiers of Porter's V Corps across the Potomac establishing a beachhead near Shepherdstown after capturing four Confederate cannons, Porter's green, untried troops were driven back across the river. This was the last skirmish of the Battle of Antietam. After the brief engagement with Porter and an evaluation of the condition of his army, Lee determined that their ability to continue the invasion of the North was not possible.

Chapter 8

The Aftermath

With Lee back in Virginia, McClellan remained in Maryland. Unlike most successful engagements, no congratulatory telegram was sent to General McClellan by President Lincoln. Lacking the praise he thought warranted, General McClellan wrote to his wife, "I feel some little pride in having with a beaten and demoralized army defeated Lee so utterly & saved the North so completely. Well—one of these days history will I trust do me justice."[116]

General McClellan went about his role to nurse his army back to health, while remaining in position to prevent Lee from renewing any new offensive in Maryland or Pennsylvania. Meanwhile, Lee was receiving accolades from Richmond for a well-won victory.[117]

The Army of the Potomac was damaged but remained a formidable force. The battlefield leadership of a wounded General Hooker was ensured. His subordinate General George Meade performed with his usual competence. Alpheus Williams performed as an adequate replacement in the XII Corps after the fatal wounding of General Mansfield. Edwin Sumner's II Corps suffered more than 40 percent of Union casualties, with Sumner demonstrating poor leadership. General Burnside chose only to execute the letter of his orders, demonstrating no creativity or initiative. General Franklin's VI Corps had little impact on the battle, and General Porter's V Corps remained mostly in reserve, except for the Battle of Shepherdstown, September 19–20. General Porter appeared to be the sole confidant of General McClellan throughout the battle. General

Pleasonton's cavalry performed few cavalry duties, suffering only thirty casualties in engagements,[118] limiting most of its activities to rounding up stragglers and sitting in reserve.

If victory in battle is defined as the army that remains in control of the battlefield, the Union could claim victory. If soundly defeating the adversary is the measure, the battle was a draw. If escaping a desperate situation to fight another day is success, the Confederacy could claim victory.[119] General McClellan bragged of his victory that thirty-nine Confederate colors and 6,000 prisoners had been obtained by the Union at South Mountain and Antietam, with not a single color lost by the Union.[120]

President Lincoln needed a military victory to quiet his critics and to allow him to issue the Emancipation Proclamation. The Battle of Antietam provided Lincoln with that win. On September 22, 1862, he released his Preliminary Emancipation Proclamation, which was to take effect on January 1, 1863. The proclamation would forever change the Civil War and the future of the country.

In Europe, both England and France had been watching the progress of the war with great interest. The argument over the availability of Southern cotton versus the question of slavery was central in the discussions. The issue of the Emancipation Proclamation settled the issue of slavery. Clearly slavery was now a major issue in the American Civil War. With the European powers' strong aversion to slavery, the conflict for the support of the Confederacy in Europe grew. Many thought that the Emancipation Proclamation would end the debate over British and French support of the Confederacy; however, this did not happen. In the fall of 1862, Emperor Napoleon III of France proposed that England and France intervene in the American conflict. In England, Lord Russell, British Foreign Minister, voiced concern that the Emancipation Proclamation would lead to a greater bloody conflict. Others thought that it would be ineffective and have no impact on the war. The government only reconsidered its position after public outcry. In early 1863, the Napoleon III proposal began to unravel. While both England and France refused to officially recognize the Confederacy, to a great extent based on the slavery issue, both continued to support the South with supplies and armaments throughout the war. In Europe, the issue of the Emancipation Proclamation made official recognition of the Confederacy politically impossible.

McClellan warned the president that radical positions on slavery would be detrimental to the army. He believed that the issue of the Emancipation Proclamation would be negatively received by the Army of the Potomac.

Abraham Lincoln with Major General George McClellan at Antietam. *Library of Congress.*

Rumors abounded in and around the army that this would be a serious problem for Lincoln, even including talk of a military coup. These rumors reached Washington. General McClellan continued to maintain his defensive positions in Maryland requesting additional logistic support. He made no efforts to pursue Lee after Porter crossed the Potomac on September 20. McClellan's supporters maintain that remaining at Antietam was appropriate. The position provided better access to Hagerstown, rather than crossing the Potomac and pursuing Lee's rear. Supporters believe this was the best defense against any attempt by Lee to enter Pennsylvania.

On October 2, 1862, Lincoln arrived at McClellan's headquarters to meet with the general and review the Union forces. Unfortunately, no third-party record was kept of the four-day visit by Lincoln. McClellan believed that Lincoln was pushing for premature pursuit of Lee. He also commented that he thought he had a positive meeting with Lincoln. Lincoln, on the other hand, found McClellan immobile and felt that the Army of the Potomac was not a fighting force, but simply McClellan's bodyguard. Ultimately, Lincoln was assessing the ability and willingness of McClellan to effectively and aggressively pursue and destroy the Confederate army. On October 6, McClellan received orders from General Halleck to cross the Potomac and engage Confederate forces. What followed was an exchange of telegraph messages between McClellan and Halleck, with Halleck demanding movement and engagement and McClellan demanding additional resources and informing Washington that he was facing unusually large enemy forces.[121] For every reason McClellan offered for not being more aggressive, the same could be said of the mobile Lee: men were totally fatigued from the fighting; units were scattered and disorganized; food and supplies were lacking; ammunition, especially artillery shells, was in short supply; and the Confederate army suffered from a lack of reinforcements. Both sides were engaged in resupply and reinforcements during this period. McClellan's actions after Antietam were questioned by Lincoln in a telegram on October 13 from the president to McClellan. This long message clearly reflected Lincoln's dissatisfaction with actions of McClellan since September 17. The message included questioning McClellan's "overcautiousness" and excuses given to General Halleck for failure to pursue Lee.[122]

By October 26, 1862, McClellan had begun moving his Army of the Potomac across into Virginia. It was not until November 2 that the last of the widely dispersed Army of the Potomac crossed the Potomac River. Lee had made the crossing with his army in one day. Most of General Lee's command was long gone from the Antietam area.

Lincoln was displeased with McClellan for his failure to pursue Lee's army after Antietam and his constant demands for additional men and supplies. Concerned about the reaction of the Army of the Potomac to any replacement, Lincoln, during his visit to McClellan in early October, determined that while McClellan was popular with the troops, a move to replace him was possible. Concerned that any immediate action might affect the election results, Lincoln waited to act until after the November election to replace McClellan. The Republican Party retained its majority in Congress after the November elections, although this majority was significantly reduced.

Finally, on November 5, President Lincoln relieved General McClellan of command and appointed thirty-eight-year-old General Ambrose Burnside to replace the thirty-six-year-old commander. Receiving the order on the seventh, George B. McClellan was sent home to Trenton, New Jersey, to await orders that never came. The selection of Burnside was made by Lincoln largely because Burnside was considered a protégé of McClellan's, not because Lincoln believed he was a better commander than others. His reticence on Burnside's ability proved to be true, and thus began Lincoln's search for a commander of U.S. forces that lasted through three more commanders of the Army of the Potomac until March 1864, when U.S. Grant was named lieutenant general in charge of all Union forces.

Meanwhile, with the leisurely response of the Union forces, General Lee and the Army of Northern Virginia were enjoying a recuperation from the events at Antietam. Replacements and resupplies were received, and the Shenandoah Valley provided a bounty of food and forage. Perhaps in anticipation of another movement into Pennsylvania, Lee began to move his command northwest to Martinsburg, Virginia, and sent General Stuart north toward Hagerstown.

By October 10, with the addition of stragglers and some replacements from Richmond, the Army of Northern Virginia would remain in the Shenandoah Valley with a present-for-duty 64,000 men, nearly double his troops at the end of the Battle of Antietam. Lee sent 1,000 cavalrymen, under J.E.B. Stuart, across the Potomac River near Williamsport to Chambersburg, Pennsylvania, some twenty miles in McClellan's rear. On October 12, Stuart escaped the pursuit of the Union and crossed the Potomac to safety.[123] This raid would add to Lincoln's frustration that McClellan was unable or unwilling to maintain control in his sector.[124] On October 28, Lee ordered Longstreet south to Culpeper Court House, while Jackson was to stay in the Shenandoah to harass McClellan's lines of communication.

Between October and December 1862, Lee increased his army from about 65,000 to more than 78,000. Unconcerned about the willingness of his adversary to reengage in conflict, Lee was confident in his ability to meet and ultimately defeat whoever had command of the Army of the Potomac. Lee continued to believe that winning a decisive battle against Union forces was necessary to win the war.

Subsequent victories at Fredericksburg (December 1862) and Chancellorsville (May 1863) restored the fighting ability of the Army of Northern Virginia and its commander. With these successes, General Lee again believed that a battle could be waged on Northern soil with the result being the annihilation of the Union army. The implementation of this plan culminated in the Battle of Gettysburg in July 1863.

Chapter 9

IMPACT ON THE WAR

S ome believe it is impossible to support the position that the ultimate
result of the Civil War was foretold by actions during and immediately
after the Battle of Antietam in the fall of 1862. Primary support for
this belief is that the war continued for more than two and a half years
after this battle. Victories at Gettysburg and Vicksburg in July 1863 and
Sherman's capture of Atlanta in September 1864 were pivotal in the war.
However, they would never have occurred if the events at Antietam had not
taken place as they did.

GENERAL GEORGE B. McCLELLAN: THE RESULTS

Regardless of one's opinion of General McClellan as a military commander,
it is clear that he was a patriot who wanted the American Dream to continue.
George McClellan was a complex, vain and ambitious man in complex
circumstances. He fought the Confederacy to, at least, a draw, at the peak
of the South's military efficiency in a political environment that challenged
his views. In spite of mixed results of his military experience, Lincoln twice
called on him to lead the most important command in the Union. Some
believe that he was not given sufficient opportunity to prove his ability as a
commander. With only staff experience in the Mexican-American War and
his engineering career, he was required to learn on the run as a commander

of a large army. He, however, was not alone with this problem during the war. Lee, Grant and nearly all senior officers had little command experience before the Civil War. They all learned on the run. Grant, however, had an opportunity to develop in lower command positions.

A comparison with General Grant is inevitable. Both had positive service in the Mexican-American War, and both left the military after that experience. Grant had two significant successes in his first two years of his return to Union service (Fort Donelson and Shiloh); McLellan had one, Antietam, and another less successful, the Peninsula Campaign. Both had conflicts with superiors—Grant with Halleck and McClellan with Stanton, Lincoln and Halleck as well. McClellan was cashiered after two years of service. Grant was under great pressure from detractors during his first two years as a general. Grant was vilified by the "Lost Cause" movement that McClellan escaped. Northern historians supported the image of Grant and ignored any positive traits of McClellan. In the end, Grant was a winner and McClellan was a defeated Democratic presidential candidate. A truly great military leader is often considered to be a general who is willing to take risks. McClellan was unwilling to take significant risks. With this failure, he cannot be considered a great commander.[125]

There is no question that General McClellan was excellent in training and organizing the Army of the Potomac and that President Lincoln saw no alternative but to reappoint him commander after the disaster of the Second Battle of Bull Run. Nonetheless, the shortcomings of General McClellan, perceived by Lincoln, during the Peninsula Campaign, amplified by the Battle of Antietam, sealed his fate and initiated the long search for a commander who could whip Bobby Lee. President Lincoln finally determined that McClellan's shortcomings were uncorrectable and that action was required.

A broad historical consensus has condemned General McClellan as an inept commander who was only of value as an organizer and trainer of a large army. Historians point out that command traits identified and accepted by President Lincoln leading to McClellan's ouster from the Army of the Potomac were justified. Clearly, as Commander-in-Chief, Lincoln had the authority to replace his generals whenever he thought it appropriate. While McClellan's performance rated between average to mediocre, he was not the unredeemable commander portrayed in much of the Civil War literature.[126]

Today, there are historians who are closely analyzing McClellan's actions and justifying his behavior. McClellan supporters excuse the command shortcomings of the general entering, conducting and following up the Battle of Antietam with reasons that range from weak to plausible. They reason that his lack of aggression is justified given the new, untrained troops, and his unwillingness to move when ordered was due to the lack of equipment and supplies. Frequently, supporters of McClellan believe that the general was simply misunderstood. His plans were more than adequate, movements appropriate and needs real. These supporters fail to accept the facts clearly demonstrated at Antietam and during the Peninsula Campaign of continuing command shortcomings that affected the engagements. His supporters point out that one of his greatest negatives was that he was a Democrat. Yet Lincoln accepted the inept Democrat generals Banks and Butler through nearly the end of the war. On September 22, McClellan sent Allen Pinkerton to visit Lincoln, fearing that the president was being influenced by McClellan's enemies. Pinkerton reported to McClellan that Lincoln had a high opinion of the general and was fully supportive.[127] Frequently, historians and military contemporaries of McClellan's are quoted to support his actions. Many historians such as Stephen Sears, Bruce Catton, James McPherson and James Murfin, as well as military officers including Ambrose Burnside, Edwin Sumner and Frances W. Palffrey, who were critical of McClellan are discounted.[128]

These supporters are led by Joseph L. Harsh, James G. Randall, Steven Stotelmyer, Tom Clemens and others. They base their positions on their analyses of the actions of McClellan and the circumstances of his commands. As a result, the positions of the McClellan supporters are their personal interpretation based on information available. Neither the modern supporters nor detractors of McClellan were at his battles, none knows his deepest thoughts and none can adequately distill the self-serving reports of those who were there. Each opinion has merit, and each should be respected.

Results of McClellan's profile of command and evaluation can be seen in the following categories.

FAILURE TO UNDERSTAND THE PURPOSE OF HIS ARMY: During the Peninsula Campaign, McClellan's objective was to capture the Confederate capital of Richmond, Virginia. At Antietam, his objectives were to protect Washington, D.C., and Baltimore, deny Lee's movement into Pennsylvania and drive the Army of Northern Virginia south across the Potomac River. Once Washington, D.C., and Baltimore were protected, President Lincoln and his administration placed importance on pressuring and defeating Confederate forces as the primary objective of the Union army. In a telegram to McClellan on September 15, after the victory at South Mountain, President Lincoln wrote (emphasis added), "Your dispatch of to-day received, God bless you and all with you! *Destroy the rebel army, if possible.*" Lincoln's approach to the war was evolving from conciliation to return the Confederacy to the Union to destroying the Confederate military might. Lincoln believed that McClellan could never understand or accept this concept. McClellan had, as his goal, to protect the North from the Rebel hordes and keep his army in pristine condition. Despite several announcements that he would attack and destroy[129] the enemy, he rarely employed his large army to achieve these boasts. This flaw was reflected in his movement of troops and their deployment in the face of the enemy.

Supporters of McClellan maintain that he accomplished his objectives at Antietam, justifying his subsequent delays in employing his army, and his actions during the Peninsula Campaign were rationalized by his supporters as a result of the lack of support by McDowell, based on Lincoln's decisions. The pressure placed on Washington, D.C., and the Shenandoah Valley by the Confederates, especially by "Stonewall" Jackson, is discounted. Others argue that the Peninsula Campaign was a success, as McClellan relocated his base at the expense of the Confederacy.

ANTAGONISTIC TOWARD AUTHORITY: Throughout McClellan's career as a Civil War senior commander, he held his superiors in contempt. He frequently complained of their incompetence and expressed disdain for the leadership of President Lincoln, Secretary Stanton and General Halleck. Most of his comments were made in private; however, his direct actions when communicating with his superiors reflected this attitude. McClellan's superiors recognized his exceptional opinion of himself, ranging from his refusal to meet with his superiors,[130] public and private comments reflected in written military orders and his comments when meeting superiors. McClellan's bold written statement to Secretary Stanton that the administration, and not himself, was responsible for the defeat in the Peninsula Campaign clearly showed his disdain for Lincoln and the administration. McClellan always doubted Lincoln's ability to rise above petty politics.[131] As military shortcomings became apparent to Lincoln, Stanton and Halleck, this antagonism added to their desire to replace him. Too frequently, historians supplement the personal views of McClellan with information from letters written to his wife, Mary Ellen, as a basis for his public persona. They fail to acknowledge that these letters became public well after the war was over.

Supporters of McClellan find his contempt for the Lincoln administration justified based on political intrigue, micromanaging and distain for his

Democratic politics. Justified or not, McClellan must have understood the price he was paying for this action. As a subordinate, such action by McClellan was certain to reflect negatively on his reputation with his superiors. Unfortunately, his public and private anti-administration statements, coupled with his military performance, made his continued acceptance by Lincoln virtually impossible.

Civilian control of the military has frequently rankled military leaders—one can see this conflict clearly play out in the contest between MacArthur and Truman and others. This civilian control of the military is fundamental to our democracy, and military leaders are expected to understand and respect this concept.[132]

THE ENEMY IS TOO STRONG: McClellan consistently overestimated the strength of the enemy. His intelligence chief, Allan Pinkerton, Chicago detective, who knew McClellan through their railroad days, usually doubled or tripled the strength of the enemy. In the Peninsula Campaign, the Confederates had fewer troops than Pinkerton's estimate of 150,000. At Harrison's Landing, after the Seven Days Battle, and after he was refused 50,000 additional forces, McClellan estimated Rebel forces at 400,000. Pinkerton had nothing to do with troop estimates at Antietam, yet his legacy and influence remained. Likewise, at Antietam, even with Special Orders No. 191, which listed units and not unit strength, McClellan estimated Lee's army at more than twice its actual numbers. These constant overestimations played into McClellan's cautious nature and resulted in his failure to take advantage of field opportunities. Modern historians who support McClellan's actions are unable to justify these overestimates. The common response was that he received this information from his cavalry and intelligence staff. They fail to comment on others who questioned these estimates or the simple math available to assess enemy strength. When Lee began his march into Maryland, he flaunted that movement to the U.S. Signal Station at Sugarloaf Mountain by marching easily within view of the station. With the ability to signal Washington, the station sent the first message of Lee's movement at 4:00 p.m. on September 4, 1862.[133] It is likely that the station saw fewer than 100,000 troops moving. There is no evidence that either McClellan or Pinkerton considered this information. Further, there are no indications that McClellan ever believed that the troop estimates could be in error. There is no indication, should he have retained his command, that he would have discontinued overestimating enemy strength.

The consistent overestimation of enemy strength likely contributed to McClellan being slow to move and very cautious in his maneuvers and attacks. If McClellan truly believed that he was always outnumbered, many of his actions are justified. Slow movement, timid employment of troops and the constant demand for more men and equipment can be attributed to this overestimation of the enemy. Yet it is difficult to understand how he accepted estimates of enemy strength twice that of the actual counts. It is possible that General McClellan wanted to conduct his engagements opposing superior forces. The overestimation of the enemy was compatible with McClellan's personality. If he was opposed by a superior force and defeated them, he could claim to truly be the "Young Napoleon." If he lost to an overwhelming enemy, then others could be blamed.[134]

HE HAS THE "SLOWS": President Lincoln and several cabinet members identified this trait before and during the Peninsula Campaign Whether this was a realistic analysis or political impatience is open to debate. The president's perception was real. McClellan's propensity to be cautious was seen in his first campaign in 1861, when he commented not to move until "everything is ready."[135] He was commanded to support General Pope at the Second Battle of Bull Run. He sent General Fitz John Porter, in support, arriving well after the battle was started. Units under General Franklin and General Sumner were dispatched too late to support Pope. Other units of McClellan's army were within marching distance of Pope during the battle. General Porter, who thought Pope an "ass," failed to follow the attack orders of Pope on August 29, 1862, and therefore his corps did not fully participate in the engagement. This resulted in Porter being court-martialed and cashiered in November 1862. In 1886, Porter's verdict was reversed based on information regarding the presence of General Longstreet before Porter's unit. This was probably not known to Porter at the time of his inaction. Supporters of McClellan point to the vindication of General Porter nearly twenty-five years after the event as justification for McClellan's lack of support of Pope. Hindsight after twenty-five years forgives many sins. The action of Porter and slow response by McClellan to support Pope is attributed to McClellan sulking at Pope's command of some of McClellan's troops and the refusal of Lincoln to provide McClellan more troops. On July 22, McClellan wrote to his wife, "The Pope bubble is likely to be suddenly collapsed...will in less than a week be in full retreat or badly whipped."[136]

McClellan pursued Lee from the Washington, D.C., area to South Mountain for about thirty-six miles. It took the army six days to cover that distance, an average of six miles per day. This was a minimal march for an army where marches of eleven to twelve miles per day were typical. McClellan excusers argue that some of the army marched faster and some slower, but the fact remains that it took six days to get units in position. In his memoirs, General Longstreet commented that McClellan was "slow and cautious" in his pursuit of Lee.[137] Another excuse used was the poor quality of roads, yet the army marched over three different satisfactory roads in good weather to Frederick. The argument that they followed one after another corps is not true. McClellan's organization of three wings provided the ability to move on three axes of advance. Another basis for his slow movement that has some merit is McClellan's first objective of protecting Washington, D.C., and Baltimore—thus his orders to Burnside's wing to move to the north to protect Baltimore rather than west toward Lee. Burnside's movement, however, does not justify slow movement by the remainder of McClellan's forces to Frederick and General Lee.

After receiving the lost Special Orders No. 191 at 1:00 p.m. on September 13, McClellan waited nearly fourteen hours before ordering movement of a majority of his troops to the gaps in South Mountain, the entry to the dispersed Rebel army. McClellan's orders on September 13 were published at 6:45 p.m. at the earliest. Supporters argue that McClellan acted with appropriate speed. Yet most of the movement ordered was for the morning of the September 14. General Pleasonton's cavalry had pushed Stuart's Confederate cavalry back from Turner's Gap. Reports were sent back to McClellan that the enemy was in retreat to Turner's Gap.[138] Pleasonton, had he been ordered, could have occupied Turner's Gap before D.H. Hill's division arrived.[139] The McClellan supporters quote Lee as reporting that McClellan moved fast and acted aggressively. They fail to note that Lee's comments appear to relate only to Pleasonton's actions. McClellan supporters also maintain that McClellan did not delay fourteen hours before taking action. This is technically true. However, except for Burnside and Franklin's Corps movement toward South Mountain and Frederick and Reno's movement to Middletown, his only general movement orders, except Pleasonton, were scheduled for the next morning. General Franklin's VI Corps received orders after 6:00 p.m. on September 13 to move the twelve miles to the summit at Crampton's Gap to engage McLaws first thing the next morning. McClellan told Franklin about receiving Special Orders No. 191 but failed to show any need for haste. Franklin's command was well rested, not having engaged the enemy since the Peninsula Campaign, and could have begun his march earlier, had he received orders or conducted a night march toward Crampton's Gap on a good road in good weather. Such a move would likely have resulted in an early victory and perhaps relief of the beleaguered troops at Harper's Ferry.

Historians have speculated that had the situation of the Lost Orders been reversed, General Lee would have immediately dispatched "Stonewall" Jackson to engage the enemy.[140] Modern historians have voiced the opinion that McClellan, in fact, moved as rapidly as possible to South Mountain. This is essentially true since his movement, while slow, was faster than Lee believed McClellan would move.[141]

McClellan's forces were successful at Turner's, Fox's and Crampton's Gaps on the evening of September 14.[142] Yet he made no attempt to take advantage of this victory by pressing the retreating Confederate forces. It took two precious days to prepare for the battle at Sharpsburg. Supporters maintain that McClellan was justified to move slowly to possibly avoid a costly battle at a location not of his choice. They point out that McClellan had, effectively, stopped Lee from entering Pennsylvania, accomplishing one of his goals, and that Lee was unlikely to take a stand with his back to the Potomac.

After the battle ended on September 17, McClellan, who clearly had the advantage in available troops, failed to attack the badly damaged Confederates who remained near Sharpsburg with their back to the Potomac River and with only one ford available to them. His excuse that his troops were spent fails to acknowledge the nearly 20,000 troops who had not been engaged in the battle and approximately 5,000 who were arriving. His supporters offer the further excuse that these were new, untried troops. This fails to account for the movement and engagement on the way to the battle. In addition, many claim that Porter's V Corps had a substantial number of untried troops. Yet fifteen of the nineteen units assigned to Porter were part of his command during the Peninsula Campaign. Of the four new regiments, the 118th Pennsylvania and 20th Maine were organized in August 1862 and the 32nd Massachusetts was organized in June 1862. The 2nd District of Columbia was organized in February 1862, probably adequately trained and had participated in the defense of Washington, D.C., prior to joining Porter. The comments that Porter's troops were too green to be engaged lacks factual support. It is estimated that only 15 percent of McClellan's troops engaged were new with little training. The 208th New York, 14th Connecticut and 130th Pennsylvania, all untrained regiments in Dwight Morris's brigade, were in action at the Sunken Road under the command of General French. They performed poorly but had seen "the elephant." The inclusion of new and marginally trained troops in engaged units was common in both armies throughout the war. Even McClellan, in his autobiography, indicated that new troops "fought like veterans, and fought well...entitled to great credit."[143] Effective commanders were aware of troop experience and managed their troops to minimize the impact of new troops on the action and the action on new troops.

A review by his supporters of McClellan's actions justifies his delay in following Lee. Consider that by remaining in Maryland, McClellan was meeting his second objective, prohibiting Lee from entering Pennsylvania. Lee had moved northwest from Antietam rather than directly south. McClellan mentioned to General Halleck in his communication of September 27 that he was securing Harper's Ferry and watching if Lee crossed the river.[144] Lee had dispatched J.E.B. Stuart north toward Hagerstown. These movements indicated possible renewal of Lee's objective to move north into Pennsylvania. There was only question remaining: Could the same objective have been met by pursuing the severely damaged Army of Northern Virginia rather than allowing Lee to resupply in the Shenandoah Valley?

Despite the urging and ordering from Washington, D.C., McClellan finally began moving his troops in pursuit of Lee on October 26, nearly three weeks after Lee left Maryland Again McClellan offered excuses ranging from needing shoes for his men to horses being too spent to move. Supporters of McClellan justify this inaction by the general as remaining at Antietam to prohibit Lee from renewing his invasion. This has some justification, except that McClellan knew by October 24 that Lee was marshalling his troops at Winchester, Virginia.[145] Except for some movement of limited troops toward Hagerstown, McClellan did not make it clear that his reason for remaining in the Antietam area was to prohibit Lee's movement north. In fact, if that was his objective, he could have moved closer to Hagerstown to accomplish that goal.

The failure to move rapidly and engage the enemy with continued pressure was a significant flaw in McClellan's tactical approach. The subsequent commander, General U.S. Grant, demonstrated that keeping pressure on General Lee was needed to prevail.

NEVER ENOUGH MEN: McClellan reported that he could use 50,000 more troops to restart the Peninsula Campaign when he was ordered to return to Washington in support of General Pope. Even before the Peninsula Campaign, McClellan demanded more and more men to meet his military objectives. When Lincoln required nearly 30,000 troops under General

McDowell to protect Washington, D.C., McClellan knew of the withholding of troops before the campaign, bristled and later blamed the failure of the campaign on insufficient men. McClellan supporters believe the general was justified in demanding additional troops, since Lincoln had significantly reduced the army's effectiveness. They fail to mitigate McClellan's demands by the fact that the Union forces were nearly twice those available to Lee.

At Antietam, McClellan had adequate troops; however, in his opinion, to pursue Lee additional troops and supplies would have been needed.

ALWAYS SHORT OF SUPPLIES: Regardless of materials and supplies available to McClellan, it was never enough. Delays in movement during the Peninsula Campaign were often attributed to a lack of supplies. After Antietam, McClellan constantly harped on the lack of supplies to General Halleck and Quartermaster General Meigs. The exchange of telegraphs between the three between October 1 and October 26, 1862,[146] showed significant arguments between them on the status of supplies. On the one hand, McClellan insisted that supplies were not received, while Halleck and Meigs insisted that all requisitions had been filled and shipped to either Harper's Ferry or Hagerstown. The answer is probably somewhere in between. Likely some supplies were delayed by train transportation and likely some had arrived and had not been distributed. During this time, Washington questioned why McClellan was not moving. Halleck suggested that McClellan cross the Potomac to be closer to Washington, D.C., and to shorten the supply lines. McClellan again stated that he could not move for lack of supplies, especially shoes. He also repeatedly demanded additional bridges connecting Harper's Ferry, even though shipments were being delivered with some delays by wagon across the pontoon bridge. He did not indicate that his present location was important to prohibiting Lee's movement north.

It is difficult to justify McClellan remaining at Antietam for want of supplies when Lee's decimated army moved into Virginia depending on a fractured line of communication. McClellan's desire to have parade ground–ready troops with no unfilled needs was impractical and resulted in his stagnation in the face of the enemy. McClellan supporters believe that the army could not move without additional logistic support, even though the Union supply line was substantially shorter than that of the moving Confederates. Other supporters indicate that McClellan wanted to stay in the Sharpsburg area to be able to pursue Lee if Lee attempted to reenter Maryland. If this was McClellan's position, he did not communicate it to any of his subordinates.

POOR TACTICAL EMPLOYMENT OF AVAILABLE TROOPS: At Antietam, McClellan's tactical plan was simple and could have been effective with better communications with commanders and adequate reconnaissance of the battlefield. For unknown reasons, McClellan did not task his cavalry commander General Pleasonton with reconnoitering the area, including fording sites along Antietam Creek.

The battle plan was to begin the assault on the Union right with General Hooker, while General Burnside, on the left, demonstrated at the Burnside Bridge to prevent Lee from moving forces from his right to left in support of "Stonewall" Jackson. After the initial attack with the XII Corps under Mansfield, added units from Sumner's II Corps would attack in the center. Porter's V Corps and the cavalry, along with Franklin's VI Corps arriving from Pleasant Valley near Harper's Ferry, would then provide the finishing blow to the Rebels.

This plan required effective command leadership, communications and timing. Orders to commanders from McClellan were verbal, brief and slow, leaving little time for preparation by the corps commanders. The lack of written orders deprived historians of the details to properly evaluate McClellan's plans. Loss of communications, including McClellan remaining in the rear, east of Antietam Creek at the Pry House, resulted in corps being employed piecemeal, allowing Lee to defend his left, center and right individually as McClellan's troops attacked each area of the battle front. Extremely poor communications with General Burnside and a total lack of reconnaissance by Pleasonton, Burnside and Cox, as well as delay of the attack from 10:00 a.m. to after 1:00 p.m., allowed Lee to move supporting forces from his right to the left without a challenge. The delay also allowed additional time for A.P. Hill to arrive from Harper's Ferry. The late initial success on the Union left by Burnside was countered by the arrival of A.P. Hill's division. Had the Burnside attack proceeded as initially planned, it is likely that Lee's right would have been rolled up prior to Hill's arrival. Considering the troop advantage for McClellan, a broad frontal attack, rather than an attack in echelon, would have placed serious pressure on Lee.

Even with this poor tactical application of the battle by McClellan, there were opportunities to employ reserve forces to continue the attack in the afternoon. The exact number of available uncommitted troops after the initial battle can be debated. However, it is difficult to justify that there were only nominal troops available to McClellan. General Lee had received serious losses during the morning and early afternoon. Union troops had nearly gained Harper's Ferry Road in front of Sharpsburg. Lee was consolidating his troops on either side of Sharpsburg, with virtually no reserves to support his forces. McClellan could have devastated the Army of Northern Virginia with a push by his reserves. He refused to deploy them, as they were his only reserves.

Lee had fought McClellan to a standstill with fewer soldiers, using tactical movement of his troops to meet the piecemeal employment of McClellan's forces. By some measures, Antietam was as much a Confederate victory as a Union victory. Certainly, news media in both the North and South declared victory. The Antietam result was in the eyes of the beholder.

Today, some historians justify his tactical plan and failure to engage his reserves on two factors: (1) The Army of the Potomac was three separate commands cobbled together after the Second Battle of Bull Run and lacked time to properly prepare for coordinated operations, and (2) A significant number of troops were new and poorly trained and would be ineffective. Both arguments have some merit but cannot justify all the flaws in McClellan's tactical plan. Most of the Army of the Potomac organized after the Second Battle of Bull Run were the same units commanded by McClellan as before the Peninsula Campaign.

McClellan's effective plan was poorly executed, which again demonstrated his significant command shortcomings. As in the Peninsula Campaign, he committed his forces piecemeal and failed to act boldly when he obtained a tactical advantage.

Supporters of General McClellan point to his seeming aggressiveness at South Mountain, movement to attack at Sharpsburg and a sound plan for the Battle of Antietam as strong points in his actions. While these factors can be argued, it remains that the shortcomings at Antietam paralleled similar shortcomings at the Peninsulas Campaign. Apparently, McClellan had learned nothing from his earlier experience. These facts became an important part of President Lincoln's evaluation of Major General George B. McClellan.

The factors outlined here, as part of the analysis by Lincoln that these shortcomings would prohibit McClellan from being successful, are reasonable. While some accuse Lincoln of micromanaging the actions of the army, no one could argue that Lincoln had the ultimate authority and responsibility to execute the war as Commander-in-Chief. His leading advisors in the government supported his decision to relieve McClellan of command from both a military and political perspective. Ultimately, with the selection of U.S. Grant in 1864, Lincoln's decision proved proper.

President Abraham Lincoln: The Results

President Lincoln had appointed McClellan, for a second time, in command of all eastern troops, with reservations. Many in his cabinet had been opposed to the appointment, but none had an acceptable alternative. McClellan was known for excellent administrative skills and was well liked by the soldiers in his command. As a strong Democrat, he provided some stability to a tenuous political situation in the country. In addition, General Burnside, when approached about commanding the Army of the Potomac before McClellan's appointment, declined, stating that he lacked the skills to command a large army. This belief proved to be accurate after he replaced McClellan.

The defeat of Pope at Bull Run and McClellan's victory at Antietam did not change Lincoln's opinion that the continuation of a policy of conciliation was not appropriate. Lincoln also knew that this change in policy was contrary to McClellan's position.[147] It should be noted that during most of McClellan's time of service, the policy of conciliation and urging the South to return to the Union was in effect and compatible with the views of both McClellan and Lincoln.[148]

In order to issue his Emancipation Proclamation, Lincoln needed a military victory. Regardless of the degree of military success, Antietam offered the win needed, allowing the president to issue his proclamation on September 22, 1862. The declaration of a military victory at Antietam did not, in Lincoln's opinion, warrant unconditional support of General McClellan commanding Union forces. In fact, the customary congratulatory telegram from the president to the winning general was absent after Antietam. General Halleck sent a congratulatory telegram to McClellan on September 30.[149]

Lincoln needed to determine, firsthand, the capabilities of the Army of the Potomac and the usefulness of its commander. To that end, he visited Antietam on October 2, 1862, to meet with McClellan and visit the troops. What he found was a wounded but victorious army, led by a confident and conceited commander who justified any shortcoming of the battle and in the pursuit of the enemy. During the visit, President Lincoln was with Illinois friend Ozias M. Hatch at an overlook of the Army of the Potomac encampment. Lincoln asked, "Do you know what this is?" "The Army of the Potomac," replied Hatch. "So it is called," Lincoln said, "but that is a mistake, it is only McClellan's bodyguard."[150] In late October, in response to McClellan's reports of the breakdown and other deficiencies of his command's horses,[151] Lincoln replied, "[W]ill you pardon me for asking what the horses of your army have done since the battle of Antietam that fatigues anything?"[152] Supporters of McClellan point out that the cavalry had been active between Sharpsburg and Hagerstown after the battle. They believe that this reflects Lincoln's lack of military knowledge, although it is possible Lincoln's remarks were for effect, not a statement of fact. These comments reflect the president's frustration with his commander. Despite reminders of the importance of moving forward both at Antietam and during the Peninsula Campaign, McClellan continued to remain unmoved, resupplying and reorganizing his command. General Halleck expressed his frustration to Hamilton R. Gamble, provisional governor of Missouri, on October 30, 1862, when he wrote, "I am sick and tired, and disgusted with affairs here in the East. There is an immobility here that exceeds all that any man can conceive of."[153]

During his visit to Antietam, President Lincoln determined that while McClellan was well liked by his command, replacing him would not result in rebellion, as some had predicted. He left the meeting unsure of McClellan's future value and hoped that additional encouragement to pursue Lee was needed for McClellan to retain his command. On October 6, 1862, McClellan received a telegraph order from General Halleck, on the president's direction, to "cross the Potomac and give battle to the enemy."[154] This began the series of communications between McClellan and Washington, discussed earlier, regarding the inability of McClellan to move his troops without adequate supplies. Lack of supplies for McClellan's army were partially true. In addition, McClellan may have wanted to stay in Maryland to prevent Lee from reentering. While this is a popular belief, there is no indication in any communications from McClellan that this was an overriding consideration for his unwillingness to move. With continuing delays, President Lincoln was unhappy with the behavior of General McClellan, who finally began crossing the Potomac on October 26. President Lincoln relieved McClellan of command on November 5, appointing Major General Ambrose Burnside as his successor.

Lincoln's concerns about the ability of General McClellan to aggressively pursue and engage the enemy was evident at Antietam during and after the battle. The president had seen these traits after the Peninsula Campaign and during the cool support of General Pope at Bull Run by McClellan. Finding no suitable alternative, Lincoln retained McClellan in command of the Army of the Potomac until after Antietam. Lincoln summarized his concerns and his concept of the pursuit and defeat of the Confederacy in his communication with McClellan on October 13. Lincoln spoke of excess caution and questioned McClellan's ability to match Lee in mobility. Lincoln's position, as stated in this telegram, foretold the ultimate future of McClellan.[155] With careful deliberation and a firsthand visit, Lincoln evaluated the future value of General McClellan and found him lacking the commitment and skills to aggressively engage the enemy. It is impossible to fault President Lincoln for his method of evaluating McClellan. Supporters of McClellan argue that the facts were unclear and that the decision made by Lincoln was flawed. Some believe that the removal of McClellan was solely a political decision to remove a successful Democratic general. Antietam marked the beginning of the president's search for a commander who was willing to close with and destroy the Rebel army.

In evaluating the performance of the Union army at Antietam, Lincoln used all resources available to him and clearly demonstrated application of his responsibilities as Commander-in-Chief of the military.

EUROPE AND ITS SUPPORT OF THE SOUTH IN THE CIVIL WAR: Great Britain and France, along with other European countries, had been watching events unfold in America to determine their support of the Union or the Confederacy. Military setbacks by Union forces in mid-1862 had led to concerns that the war would bankrupt the Union and whether a negotiated peace was possible. To that end, British Foreign Minister John Russell and William Gladstone, along with Napoleon III of France, had been negotiating to mediate a solution between the Union and the Confederacy, to ultimately lift the Union blockade of the South and make Southern cotton available. By late October, British Prime Minister Viscount Palmerston had realized that the Confederate defeat at Antietam ended the chance for a mediated settlement. While Russell, Gladstone and Napoleon did not immediately give up their quest for a settlement, in November the British cabinet announced its opposition to involvement, leading Belgium and other European governments to quit direct support of the Confederate government. By January 1863, and the effective date of the Emancipation Proclamation, public support for the Union had resulted in the elimination of official recognition of the Confederacy by all of Europe. Both France and England would continue to support the Confederate war effort with continued hope for the availability of Southern cotton. The victory at Antietam by the Union and the issuance of the Emancipation Proclamation resolved the possibility of direct entry of Europe as allies of the Confederacy.

AMERICAN POLITICAL SCENE IN THE ELECTION OF NOVEMBER 1862: The issue of the Emancipation Proclamation, military deadlock, additional troop calls, the internal blockade, abolitionism and the suspension of *habeas corpus* were serious topics for the November 1862 elections.[156] In addition, opposition to the draft to fill troop needs, poor military results and increased guerrilla activities in border states gave the Democrats political opportunities in the election. Most important to the Democrats was emancipation. This strong opposition, with racial overtones, led to acrimonious debate leading up to the elections. Peace Democrats' opposition to the war was fueled by poor results on the field of battle by Union troops, especially in the important area around Washington, D.C. Prior to the Battle of Antietam, both Republicans and Democrats believed that Democratic control of the House of Representatives was a certainty. Republican press exaggerated the victory at Antietam as salvation for the Union. McClellan's inactivity mitigated the positive value of the Antietam victory, and the election remained in doubt. The failure of Lee to move into and remain in Pennsylvania was a significant factor during the election. Had Lee been able to stay in Pennsylvania, the outcome of the election could have been in favor of the Democrats. General McClellan must be credited with preventing Lee from meeting one of his primary objectives for the Maryland Campaign.

The elections were a modest victory for the Republicans, retaining a twenty-four-seat margin in the U.S. House of Representatives, losing thirty-four seats to the Democrats and gaining five seats in the Senate. In the Thirty-Seventh Congress, votes for Schuyler Colfax represented 55 percent of the vote, compared to 70 percent in the Thirty-Sixth Congress.[157] The Republicans retained all but two of the nineteen Northern states governorships and all but three of the state legislatures. Had there been a Confederate victory at Antietam, the results of the election might have been substantially different and the political scene for the period forever changed. The political success of the 1862 election, thanks greatly to Antietam, would carry over to the election of 1864.

The poor overall results of General McClellan at Antietam, the evaluation of the results by President Lincoln and the unprecedented impact of the Battle of Antietam and the subsequent issue of the Emancipation Proclamation changed the battle landscape of the war by the Union.

General Robert E. Lee: The Results

When the Army of Northern Virginia began its invasion of Maryland, the Confederacy was close to a total victory over a demoralized Union army. After Antietam, the Confederate armies never came close to defeating the North.

Robert E. Lee was a well-respected military leader in the U.S. Army. While he disagreed with the separation of the country, he could not raise his sword against his home state of Virginia. Operating in the Confederacy, where President Jefferson Davis was the General-in-Chief of the army, Lee was limited in his influence on command decisions outside his immediate assignment. He had little influence over any military activities outside the Army of Northern Virginia. Without a command, Lee was military advisor to President Davis until June 1862. His reputation grew after he replaced the wounded General Joseph Johnston during General McClellan's Peninsula Campaign. Except for significant losses at Malvern Hill, Lee was successful in driving McClellan from near Richmond to Harrison's Landing during the Peninsula Campaign. Further success at the Second Battle of Bull Run enhanced his reputation. Dividing his troops against General Pope disrupted Union plans, resulting in confusion and a disorganized attack by Pope. The Battle of Antietam was considered a draw by the Confedcracy, as a small army fought McClellan to a stand still and escaped to Virginia, and this did nothing to diminish Lee's reputation. Subsequent to Antietam, military success against the inept and outmatched General Burnside and General Hooker only increased the invincibility myth of General Lee. His defeat at Gettysburg and subsequent losses to General Grant were the only blots on his résumé. Even these defeats were rationalized as the gasps of a Confederacy without enough men and material.

Postwar "Lost Cause" doctrine cemented General Robert E. Lee as the preeminent general in the Civil War and perhaps the greatest general in U.S. history. The Pulitzer Prize–winning *R.E. Lee*, written in 1935 by Douglas Southall Freeman, is an excellent example of a well-written four volume work that found no faults with Lee. Freeman was the son of a Confederate veteran.[158] Justifying the loss by the God-fearing South to the heathen North required creating heroes, such as Lee, and villains, like Grant.

Even with these accolades, General Lee demonstrated deficiencies at Antietam that would ultimately contribute to the defeat of the Confederate army.

POOR STRATEGIC SENSE: From a broad strategic perspective, the invasion of Maryland, in Lee's judgment, would bring both political and recruiting support to the Confederacy. In fact, Confederate forces were received coolly by the Maryland population. Recruiting from Maryland was nonexistent. Even farmers and possible suppliers of goods for the Confederate army refused to receive payment in Confederate currency or notes. In spite of the invasion by the Army of Northern Virginia, Maryland remained safely in the Union.

Lee may have been overly optimistic that a success on Union soil would immediately bring England, France and other European nations to officially recognize the Confederacy. He failed to understand that the South's position on slavery was a major impediment to official recognition. While Europe needed Southern cotton, the long-standing antislavery position of both England and France was of overriding importance to those governments.

From a military principle perspective, General Lee had a fatal flaw. He believed that the Confederacy must achieve success in major battles against the Union force. He thought that the lack of men and material compared to the Union dictated aggressive offensive action by his army. This position was contrary to that of President Davis, who believed that guerrilla warfare to wear down and tire the Union was the path to success. Clausewitz, who chronicled warfare during the Napoleonic period, emphasized that the number-one objective of war was defeating the enemy army. However, he added that defeating the enemy's will to win was a part of this objective. The difference with Lee was never addressed by Davis. This flaw of Lee's, more than any other, was a precursor to ultimate failure. Throughout his command, including before and after Antietam, Lee consistently engaged superior Union forces because they were there. His decision to fight a superior force at Antietam would be repeated time and again as the war progressed. Large losses in these head-to-head engagements could not be replaced by the limited human resources available to the South.

OVERESTIMATION OF THE CAPABILITIES OF HIS ARMY: Despite supply limitations and physical abilities of his army, Lee consistently believed his troops capable of more than they could produce. This belief was well summarized by General James Longstreet: "General Lee's confidence in the strength of his army, the situation of affairs, and the value of the moral effects upon the country, North and South, was fully manifest by the nature of the campaign he had just entered upon, especially that portion of it directed against Harper's Ferry, which, as events were soon to prove, weakened the effectiveness of his main army in the main issue, which happened to be Antietam."[159] This flaw had been apparent at Malvern Hill, in July 1862, when he attacked strong defensive positions of the Union in spite of warnings by his generals. It is possible that his defense at Antietam was based on McClellan's success at Malvern Hill. Lee likely believed that his strong defensive position at Antietam could defeat the timid McClellan.

TACTICAL DEFICIENCIES: At Antietam, Lee used movement from one side of the battle to the other to support a defense of General McClellan's echelon attack pattern. His tactical decision to stand and fight with his back to the Potomac River was an invitation to disaster, even though Lee had developed a secondary escape route along the Chesapeake & Ohio Canal. Had McClellan used the advantage he had on September 17 or attacked on September 18, it is likely Lee's army would have been destroyed and the war ended. His expensive tendency to attack because the enemy was in front of him would be repeated at Gettysburg and during actions leading to the Siege of Petersburg.

Lee also had an opportunity at Frederick of inflicting significant damage to McClellan's forces, especially when Burnside had moved his wing north to protect Baltimore. Such an attack would have slowed McClellan's advance to South Mountain, giving Lee an opportunity to continue toward Pennsylvania.[160]

COMMAND SHORTCOMINGS: General Lee was fortunate to have strong commanders such as James Longstreet and "Stonewall" Jackson. These commanders could operate with simple, mission-type orders, typical of those issued by General Lee. Lee's resolution of questions, conflicts and problems was based on a quiet, conciliatory approach. Had these subordinates not been available, Lee would have had serious command problems. His style of command was effective with leaders like Longstreet and Jackson. However, this style was much less effective on generals such as J.E.B. Stuart. Lee was known for a small, insignificant staff that was more messengers than staff officers. The loss of Special Orders No. 191 can be attributed to poor staff work of not accounting for written orders. Special Orders No. 191 itself is an example of overly simple orders for complex maneuvers. Factors such as coordination of units, overall time goals and other details were absent from the order. The time goal ordered for the capture of Harper's Ferry was unrealistic and significantly contributed to the failure of the campaign. The loss of the Special Orders can also be attributed to poor communications of special assignment. General Jackson assumed that D.H. Hill's division was part of his command when it had not been officially assigned. It is likely that a duplicate order was prepared as a result of this oversight. General Lee expected his logistic support to keep up with him and infrequently changed his tactical actions based on logistic needs. While this shortcoming was evident but minimized in the relatively static one-day battle at Antietam, it would be amplified later during the war, especially at Gettysburg and action in 1864 leading to the Siege of Petersburg.

These shortcomings of General Lee, demonstrated at Antietam, were a precursor to his continued approach to the war that ultimately resulted in victory for the Union. General Lee proved to be a general superior to many of his adversaries, but he was not the invincible leader depicted after the war.

FINAL THOUGHTS

Antietam was a turning point in the Civil War. To the public, Antietam was delivered with the first graphic photos of the horrors of war. The arrival of Alexander Gardner and James Gibson at Antietam, shortly after the battle had ended, provided the American public with their first view of war. One month after the battle, their graphic photographs were on display in their boss Mathew Brady's studio in New York. Most of the Union soldiers were already buried; seeing the photos of the unburied Confederate dead had a sobering effect on the civilian population.[161]

The "win" at Antietam provided the background for the issue of the Emancipation Proclamation, which would change the character of the war and foreclose recognition of the Confederacy by European powers. The Union victory at Antietam ensured Lincoln supporters' control of the 1862 election. That election would set the tone for Lincoln's reelection in 1864.

The actions of the primary players—Lincoln, McClellan and Lee—resulted in significant changes in command and redirection of political and military policy. After Antietam, the prevailing Union government policy of conciliation and coaxing the Confederacy back into the Union was changed to defeating the South's military ability to continue the fight. General McClellan was determined by President Lincoln to lack fighting qualities needed to defeat the Confederacy. While it took a considerable time to find the right commander, the tone of the war was changing after Antietam. General Lee, considered as successful at Antietam by the South, demonstrated command shortcomings that would contribute to the defeat of the Confederacy.

Battles that followed Antietam were important to the war but could not have happened without the Union victory at Antietam. Union military successes at Gettysburg and Vicksburg would not have been possible had the South prevailed at Antietam.

General Halleck noted in a communication on March 31, 1863, to General Grant that "[t]he character of the war has very much changed within the last year. There is now no possible hope for reconciliation with the rebels….There can be no peace but that which is forced by the sword. We must conquer the rebels or be concurred by them."[162] The realization that the Confederacy could not be coaxed back into the Union changed the dynamics of the war, making the destruction of the Southern army a primary goal. The necessity to defeat the enemy army earlier in the war was missed by General McClellan and understood but not pushed by President Lincoln. The policy of conciliation and urging the South back into the Union through 1862 hampered the actions of McClellan.

The preponderance of opinion from historians finds McClellan too conservative in politics and one who conducted operations to succeed in conflict to create change while preserving social order and political stability.[163] McClellan's philosophy, ultimately, came in conflict with the changing philosophy and policies of Lincoln. As a result, McClellan's value to the Union became expendable. His poor performance, as evaluated by Lincoln, led to his removal after Antietam and was the first step in finding a winning general. Based on military performance, Lincoln made a political and military decision to replace McClellan. There was no move by military leadership to find an assignment with the army for McClellan after his dismissal. Unlike other failed large-unit command generals (Pope, McDowell, Burnside and Hooker), McClellan had no place in the army after being relieved of command of the Army of the Potomac.

General Lee demonstrated deficiencies that would lead to his defeat when he encountered a general who was bent on defeating the Rebel army rather than keeping them at bay. His tendency to stand and fight superior enemy forces resulted in losses that the Confederacy could not replace. These factors made the Battle of Antietam the most significant engagement of the Civil War. It was a pivotal point that predicted the ultimate victory by the Union.

Appendix 1

ORDER OF BATTLE
UNION AND CONFEDERATE

T his is the order of battle as of September 17–18, 1862, compiled from Antietam Battlefield Board, *Atlas of the Battlefield of Antietam* and *OR*, ser. 1, vol. 19, pt. 1, pages 169–80 and 803–10. Officers killed or wounded at South Mountain, such as Jesse Reno (k), Union IX Corps, are not included. A "( )" indicates officer casualties in the form of "(k)" for killed, "(w)" for wounded and "(mw)" for mortally wounded.

ARMY OF POTOMAC

Major General George B. McClellan

CAVALRY DIVISION—BRIGADIER GENERAL ALFRED PLEASONTON
1st Brigade—Major Charles Whiting
5th United States
6th United States

2nd Brigade—Colonel John F. Farnsworth
8th Illinois
3rd Indiana
1st Massachusetts

3rd Brigade—Colonel Richard H. Rush
4th Pennsylvania
6th Pennsylvania

4th Brigade—Colonel Andrew T. McReynolds
1st New York
12th Pennsylvania

5th Brigade—Colonel Benjamin F. Davis
8th New York
3rd Pennsylvania
15th Pennsylvania, Detachment (unattached)

Artillery
2nd U.S. Batteries A, B, L, M
3rd U.S. Batteries C, G

I Corps

Major General Joseph Hooker (w), Brigadier General George G. Meade

1st DIVISION—BRIGADIER GENERAL ABNER DOUBLEDAY
1st Brigade—Colonel Walter Phelps Jr.
22nd New York
24th New York
30th New York
84th New York
U.S. Sharpshooters

2nd Brigade—Lieutenant Colonel J. William Hoffman
7th Indiana
76th New York
95th New York
56th Pennsylvania

3rd Brigade—Brigadier General Marzena R. Patrick
21st New York

23rd New York
35th New York
80th New York

4th Brigade—Brigadier General John Gibbon
19th Indiana
2nd Wisconsin
6th Wisconsin
7th Wisconsin

Artillery—Captain J. Albert Monroe
New Hampshire Light 1st Battery
1st New York Light Battery L
1st Rhode Island Light Battery D
4th U.S. Battery B

2nd DIVISION—BRIGADIER GENERAL JAMES B. RICKETTS
1st Brigade—Brigadier General Duryea
97th New York
104th New York
105th New York
107th Pennsylvania

2nd Brigade—Colonel William A. Christian, Colonel Peter Lyle
26th New York
94th New York
88th Pennsylvania
90th Pennsylvania

3rd Brigade—Brigadier General George L. Hartsuff (w), Colonel Richard
  Coulter
12th Massachusetts
13th Massachusetts
83rd New York
11th Pennsylvania

Artillery
1st Pennsylvania Light Battery F
Pennsylvania Light Battery C

3rd Division—Brigadier General George G. Meade, Brigadier General Truman Seymour

1st Brigade—Brigadier General Truman Seymour, Colonel R. Biddle Roberts

1st Pennsylvania
2nd Pennsylvania
5th Pennsylvania
6th Pennsylvania
13th Pennsylvania

2nd Brigade—Colonel Albert L. Magilton
3rd Pennsylvania
4th Pennsylvania
7th Pennsylvania
8th Pennsylvania

3rd Brigade—Lieutenant Colonel Robert Anderson
9th Pennsylvania
10th Pennsylvania
11th Pennsylvania
12th Pennsylvania

Artillery
1st Pennsylvania Light Batteries A, B
5th U.S. Battery C

II Corps

Major General Edwin V. Summer

1st Division—Major General Israel B. Richardson (mw), Brigadier General John C. Caldwell, Brigadier General Winfield S. Hancock

1st Brigade—Brigadier General John C. Caldwell
5th New Hampshire
7th New York
61st New York
64th New York
81st Pennsylvania

2nd Brigade—Brigadier General Thomas F. Meagher, Colonel John Burke
63rd New York
69th New York
88th New York
29th Massachusetts

3rd Brigade—John R. Brooke
2nd Delaware
52nd New York
57th New York
66th New York
53rd Pennsylvania

Artillery
1st New York Light Battery B
4th U.S. Batteries A, C

2nd DIVISION—MAJOR GENERAL JOHN SEDGWICK (W), BRIGADIER GENERAL
   OLIVER O. HOWARD
1st Brigade—Brigadier General Willis A. Gorman
15th Massachusetts, 1st Company Massachusetts Sharpshooters (attached)
1st Minnesota, 2nd Company Minnesota Sharpshooters (attached)
34th New York
82nd New York

2nd Brigade—Brigadier General Oliver O. Howard, Colonel Joshua T.
   Owen, Colonel De Witte C. Baxter
69th Pennsylvania
71st Pennsylvania
72nd Pennsylvania
106th Pennsylvania

3rd Brigade—Brigadier General N.J.T. Dana (w), Colonel Norman J. Hall
19th Massachusetts
20th Massachusetts
7th Michigan
42nd New York
59th New York

Artillery
1st Rhode Island Light Battery A
1st U.S. Battery I

3rd DIVISION—BRIGADIER GENERAL WILLIAM H. FRENCH
1st Brigade—General Nathan Kimball
14th Indiana
8th Ohio
132nd Pennsylvania
7th West Virginia

2nd Brigade—Colonel Dwight Morris
14th Connecticut
108th New York
130th Pennsylvania

3rd Brigade—Brigadier General Max Weber (w), Colonel John W. Andrews
1st Delaware
5th Maryland
4th New York

Unattached Artillery
1st New York Light Battery G
1st Rhode Island Light Batteries B, G

V Corps

Major General Fitz John Porter

1st DIVISION—MAJOR GENERAL GEORGE W. MORELL
1st Brigade—Colonel James Barnes
2nd Main
18th Massachusetts
22nd Massachusetts, 2nd Company Massachusetts Sharpshooters (attached)
1st Michigan
13th New York
25th New York
118th Pennsylvania

2nd Brigade—Brigadier General Charles Griffin
2nd District of Columbia
9th Massachusetts
32nd Massachusetts
4th Michigan
14th New York
62nd Pennsylvania

3rd Brigade—Colonel T.B.W. Stockton
16th Michigan, Brady's Company Michigan Sharpshooters (attached)
20th Maine
12th New York
17th New York
44th New York
83rd Pennsylvania

Sharpshooters
1st U.S.

Artillery
Massachusetts Light Battery C
1st Rhode Island Light Battery C
5th U.S. Battery D

2nd DIVISION—BRIGADIER GENERAL GEORGE SYKES
1st Brigade—Lieutenant Colonel Robert C. Buchanan
3rd U.S.
4th U.S.
12th U.S. 1st Battalion
12th U.S. 2nd Battalion
14th U.S. 1st Battalion
14th U.S. 2nd Battalion

2nd Brigade—Major Charles S. Lovell
1st U.S.
2nd U.S.
6th U.S.
10th U.S.
11th U.S.
17th U.S.

3rd Brigade—Colonel Gouverneur K. Warren
5th New York
10th New York

Artillery
1st U.S. Batteries E, G
5th U.S. Batteries I, K

3rd DIVISION—MAJOR GENERAL ANDREW A. HUMPHREYS
1st Brigade—Brigadier General Erastus B. Tyler
91st Pennsylvania
126th Pennsylvania
129th Pennsylvania
134th Pennsylvania

2nd Brigade—Colonel Peter H. Allabach
123rd Pennsylvania
131st Pennsylvania
133rd Pennsylvania
155th Pennsylvania

Artillery—Captain Lucius N. Robinson
1st New York Light Battery C
1st Ohio Light Battery L

Artillery Reserve—Lieutenant Colonel William Hays
1st Battalion, New York Light Batteries A, B, C, D
New York Light 5th Battery
1st U.S. Battery K
4th U.S. Battery G

VI Corps

Major General William B. Franklin

1st DIVISION—MAJOR GENERAL HENRY W. SLOCUM
1st Brigade—Colonel Alfred T.A. Torbert
1st New Jersey

2nd New Jersey
3rd New Jersey
4th New Jersey

2nd Brigade—Colonel Joseph J. Bartlett
5th Maine
16th New York
27th New York
96th Pennsylvania

3rd Brigade—Brigadier General John Newton
18th New York
31st New York
32nd New York
95th Pennsylvania

Artillery—Captain Emory Upton
Maryland Light Battery A
Massachusetts Light Battery A
New Jersey Light Battery A
2nd U.S. Battery D

2nd DIVISION—MAJOR GENERAL WILLIAM F. SMITH
1st Brigade—Brigadier General Winfield S. Hancock
Colonel Amasa Cobb
6th Maine
43rd New York
49th Pennsylvania
137th Pennsylvania
5th Wisconsin

2nd Brigade—Brigadier General W.T.H. Brooks
2nd Vermont
3rd Vermont
4th Vermont
5th Vermont
6th Vermont

3rd Brigade—Colonel William H. Irwin
7th Maine
20th New York
33rd New York
49th New York
77th New York

Artillery—Captain Romeyn B. Ayres
Maryland Light Battery B
New York Light 1st Battery
5th U.S. Battery F

1st DIVISION, IV CORPS (ATTACHED)—MAJOR GENERAL DARIUS N. COUCH
1st Brigade—Brigadier General Charles Devens Jr.
7th Massachusetts
10th Massachusetts
36th New York
2nd Rhode Island

2nd Brigade—Brigadier General Albion P. Howe
62nd New York
93rd Pennsylvania
98th Pennsylvania
102nd Pennsylvania
139th Pennsylvania

3rd Brigade—Brigadier General John Cochrane
65th New York
67th New York
122nd New York
23rd Pennsylvania
61st Pennsylvania
82nd Pennsylvania

Artillery
1st Pennsylvania Light Batteries C, D
New York Light, 3rd Battery
2nd U.S. Battery G

Appendix 1

IX Corps

Major General Ambrose E. Burnside, Brigadier General Jacob D. Cox

1st Division—Brigadier General Orlando B. Willcox
1st Brigade—Colonel Benjamin C. Christ
28th Massachusetts
17th Michigan
79th New York
50th Pennsylvania

2nd Brigade—Colonel Thomas Welsh
8th Michigan
46th New York
45th Pennsylvania
100th Pennsylvania

Artillery
Massachusetts Light 8th Battery
2nd U.S. Battery E

2nd Division—Brigadier General Samuel D. Sturgis
1st Brigade—Brigadier General James Nagle
2nd Maryland
6th New Hampshire
9th New Hampshire
48th Pennsylvania

2nd Brigade—Brigadier General Edward Ferrero
21st Massachusetts
35th Massachusetts
51st New York
51st Pennsylvania

Artillery
Pennsylvania Light Battery D
4th U.S. Battery E

3RD DIVISION—BRIGADIER GENERAL ISAAC P. RODMAN (MW), COLONEL EDWARD HARLAND
1st Brigade—Colonel Harrison S. Fairchild
9th New York
89th New York
103rd New York

2nd Brigade—Colonel Edward Harland
8th Connecticut
11th Connecticut
16th Connecticut
4th Rhode Island

Artillery
5th U.S. Battery A

KANAWHA DIVISION—COLONEL ELIAKIM P. SCAMMON
1st Brigade—Colonel Hugh Ewing
12th Ohio
23rd Ohio
30th Ohio

Artillery
Ohio Light 1st Battery

Cavalry
Gilmore's and Harrison's Company West Virginia Cavalry

2nd Brigade—Colonel George Crook
11th Ohio
28th Ohio
36th Ohio

Artillery
Kentucky Light Simmond's Battery
Cavalry—Schambeck's Company, Chicago Dragoons

Unattached Artillery
2nd New York Battery L
3rd U.S. Batteries L, M

Unattached Cavalry
6th New York (8 companies)
Ohio Cavalry, 3rd Independent Company

XII Corps

Major General Joseph K.F. Mansfield (mw), Brigadier General Alpheus S. Williams

1st Division—Brigadier General Alpheus S. Williams, Brigadier General Samuel W. Crawford (w), Brigadier General George H. Gordon
1st Brigade—Brigadier General Samuel W. Crawford, Colonel Joseph F. Knipe
10th Maine
28th New York
46th Pennsylvania
124th Pennsylvania
125th Pennsylvania
128th Pennsylvania

3rd Brigade—Brigadier General George H. Gordon, Colonel Thomas H. Ruger
27th Indiana
13th New Jersey
2nd Massachusetts, Zouaves d'Afrique (attached)
107th New York
3rd Wisconsin

2nd Division—Brigadier General George S. Greene
1st Brigade—Lieutenant Colonel Hector Tyndale (w), Major Orrin J. Crane
5th Ohio
7th Ohio
66th Ohio
28th Pennsylvania

2nd Brigade—Colonel Henry J. Stainrock
3rd Maryland
102nd New York
111th Pennsylvania

3rd Brigade—Colonel William B. Goodrich (k), Lieutenant Colonel
   Jonathan Austin
3rd Delaware
60th New York
78th New York
Purnell Maryland Legion

Corps Artillery—Captain Clermont L. Best
Main Light, 4th and 6th Batteries
1st New York Light Battery M
New York Light 10th Battery
Pennsylvania Light Batteries E, F
4th U.S. Battery F

Army of Northern Virginia

General Robert E. Lee

CAVALRY DIVISION—MAJOR GENERAL J.E.B. STUART
Hampton's Brigade—Brigadier General Wade Hampton
1st North Carolina
2nd South Carolina
Cobb's Georgia Legion
Jeff Davis Mississippi Legion

Lee's Brigade—Brigadier General Fitzhugh Lee
1st Virginia
3rd Virginia
4th Virginia
5th Virginia
9th Virginia

Robertson's Brigade—Colonel Thomas T. Munford
2nd Virginia
7th Virginia
12th Virginia

Horse Artillery—Major John Pelham
Pelham's Virginia Battery
Chew's Virginia Battery
Hart's South Carolina Battery

Reserve Artillery—Brigadier General William N. Pendleton
Cutt's Battalion—Lieutenant Colonel A.S. Cutts
Blackshears's Georgia Battery
Patterson's Georgia Battery
Irwin Georgia Artillery Lane's Battery
Ross's Georgia Battery
Lloyd's North Carolina Battery
Jones's Battalion—Major H.P. Jones
Turner's Virginia Battery
Orange Virginia Artillery Peyton's Battery
Morris Virginia Artillery Page's Battery
Wimbish's Virginia Battery
Magruder Artillery (unattached)
Cutshaw's Virginia Battery

Longstreet's Corps

Major General James Longstreet

MCLAWS'S DIVISION—MAJOR GENERAL LAFAYETTE MCLAWS
Kershaw's Brigade—Brigadier General Joseph B. Kershaw
2nd South Carolina
3rd South Carolina
7th South Carolina
8th South Carolina

Cobb's Brigade—Lieutenant Colonel C.C. Sanders, Lieutenant Colonel
  William MacRae
16th Georgia
24th Georgia
15th North Carolina
Cobb's Georgia Legion
Semmes's Brigade—Brigadier General Paul J. Semmes

10th Georgia
53rd Georgia
15th Virginia
32nd Virginia

Barksdale's Brigade—Brigadier General William Barksdale
13th Mississippi
17th Mississippi
18th Mississippi
21st Mississippi

Artillery—Colonel Henry C. Cabell
Manly's North Carolina Battery
Pulaski's Georgia Artillery
Richmond Fayette Artillery
Richmond Howitzer 1st Company
Troop Georgia Artillery

ANDERSON'S DIVISION—MAJOR GENERAL RICHARD H. ANDERSON (w),
    BRIGADIER GENERAL ROGER A. PRIOR
Wilcox's Brigade—Colonel Alfred Cumming, Major H.A. Herbert
8th Alabama
9th Alabama
10th Alabama
11th Alabama

Featherston's Brigade—Colonel Carnot Posey
12th Mississippi
16th Mississippi
19th Mississippi
2nd Mississippi Battalion

Armistead's Brigade—Brigadier General Lewis A. Armistead (w), Colonel
    J.G. Hodges
9th Virginia
14th Virginia
38th Virginia
53rd Virginia
57th Virginia

Pryor's Brigade—Brigadier General Roger A. Prior, Colonel John C.
  Hately (w)
14th Alabama
2nd Florida
5th Florida
8th Florida
3rd Virginia

Mahone's Brigade, attached to Prior's Brigade—Colonel William A. Parham
6th Virginia
12th Virginia
16th Virginia
41st Virginia
61st Virginia

Wright's Brigade—Brigadier General Ambrose R. Wright (w), Colonel
  Robert Jones (w), Colonel William Gibson
44th Alabama
3rd Georgia
22nd Georgia
48th Georgia

Artillery—Captain Cary F. Grimes (k), Major John S. Saunders
Donaldsonville Louisiana Artillery Maurin's Battery
Huger's Norfolk Battery
Moorman's Lynchburg Battery
Grimes's Portsmouth Battery

JONES'S DIVISION—BRIGADIER GENERAL DAVID R. JONES
Toombs's Brigade—Brigadier General Robert Toombs, Colonel Henry L.
  Benning
2nd Georgia
15th Georgia
17th Georgia
20th Georgia

Drayton's Brigade—Brigadier General Thomas F. Drayton
50th Georgia
51st Georgia

15th South Carolina
3rd South Carolina Battalion

Pickett's Brigade—Brigadier General Richard B. Garnett
8th Virginia
18th Virginia
19th Virginia
28th Virginia
56th Virginia

Kemper's Brigade—Brigadier General James L. Kemper
1st Virginia
7th Virginia
11th Virginia
17th Virginia
24th Virginia

Jenkin's Brigade—Colonel Joseph Walker
1st South Carolina Volunteers
2nd South Carolina Rifles
5th South Carolina
6th South Carolina
4th South Carolina Battalion
Palmetto South Carolina Sharpshooters

Anderson's Brigade—Colonel George T. Anderson
1st Georgia
7th Georgia
8th Georgia
9th Georgia
11th Georgia
Wise Virginia Artillery, J.S. Brown's Battery

WALKER'S DIVISION—BRIGADIER GENERAL JOHN G. WALKER
Walker's Brigade—Colonel Van H, Manning (w), Colonel E.D. Hall
3rd Arkansas
27th North Carolina
46th North Carolina
48th North Carolina

30th Virginia
French's Stafford Battery

Ransom's Brigade—Brigadier General Robert Ransom Jr.
24th North Carolina
25th North Carolina
35th North Carolina
49th North Carolina
Branch's Petersburg Field Artillery

HOOD'S DIVISION—BRIGADIER GENERAL JOHN B. HOOD
Hood's Brigade—Colonel William T. Wofford
18th Georgia
1st Texas
4th Texas
5th Texas
Hampton South Carolina Legion

Law's Brigade—Colonel Evander M. Law
4th Alabama
2nd Mississippi
11th Mississippi
6th North Carolina

Artillery—Major B.W. Frobel
German Charleston Artillery
Palmetto South Carolina Artillery
Rowan North Carolina Artillery

Evan's Independent Brigade—Brigadier General Nathan G. Evans,
    Colonel P.F. Stevens
17th South Carolina
18th South Carolina
22nd South Carolina
23rd South Carolina
Holcombe South Carolina Legion

Artillery
Macbeth South Carolina Artillery

Corps Artillery
1ˢᵗ Battalion—Colonel John B. Walton
Washington Louisiana Artillery 1ˢᵗ, 2ⁿᵈ, 3ʳᵈ, 4ᵗʰ Companies
2ⁿᵈ Battalion—Colonel Stephen D. Lee
Ashland Virginia Artillery
Bedford Virginia Artillery
Brooks South Carolina Artillery
Eubank's Bath Artillery
Madison Louisiana Light Artillery
Parker's Richmond Artillery

Jackson's Corps

Major General Thomas J. Jackson

EWELL'S DIVISION—BRIGADIER GENERAL ALEXANDER R. LAWTON (w),
    BRIGADIER GENERAL JUBAL A. EARLY
Lawton's Brigade—Colonel Marcellus Douglas (k), Major J.H. Lowe
13ᵗʰ Georgia
26ᵗʰ Georgia
31ˢᵗ Georgia
38ᵗʰ Georgia
60ᵗʰ Georgia
61ˢᵗ Georgia

Early's Brigade—Brigadier General Jubal A. Early, Colonel William Smith (w)
13ᵗʰ Virginia
25ᵗʰ Virginia
31ˢᵗ Virginia
44ᵗʰ Virginia
49ᵗʰ Virginia
52ⁿᵈ Virginia
58ᵗʰ Virginia

Trimble's Brigade—Colonel James A. Walker (w)
15ᵗʰ Alabama
12ᵗʰ Georgia
21ˢᵗ Georgia

21st North Carolina
1st North Carolina Battalion

Hay's Brigade—Brigadier General Harry T. Hays
5th Louisiana
6th Louisiana
7th Louisiana
8th Louisiana
14th Louisiana

Artillery—Major A.R. Courtney
Louisiana Guard Artillery D'Aquin's Battery
Staunton Virginia Artillery Balthis's Battery
Johnson's Virginia Battery

HILL'S LIGHT DIVISION—MAJOR GENERAL A.P. HILL
Branch's Brigade—Brigadier General L. O'Brien Branch (k), Colonel
    Thomas H. Lane
7th North Carolina
18th North Carolina
28th North Carolina
33rd North Carolina
37th North Carolina

Gregg's Brigade—Brigadier General Maxty Gregg
1st South Carolina, Provisional
1st South Carolina Rifles
12th South Carolina
13th South Carolina
14th South Carolina

Field's Brigade—Colonel John M. Brockenbrough
40th Virginia
47th Virginia
55th Virginia
22nd Virginia Battalion

Archer's Brigade—Brigadier General James J. Archer, Colonel Peter Turney
19th Georgia

1st Tennessee
7th Tennessee
14th Tennessee

Pender's Brigade—Brigadier General William D. Pender, Colonel R.H.
  Brewer
16th North Carolina
22nd North Carolina
34th North Carolina
38th North Carolina

Artillery—Lieutenant Colonel R.L. Walker
Fredericksburg Virginia Artillery Braxton's Battery
Pee Dee South Carolina Artillery McIntosh's Battery
Purcell Richmond Artillery Pegram's Battery
Crenshaw's Richmond Battery

JACKSON'S DIVISION—BRIGADIER GENERAL JOHN R. JONES (W), BRIGADIER
  GENERAL WILLIAM E. STARKE (K), COLONEL ANDREW J. GRIGSBY
Winder's Brigade—Colonel Andrew J. Grigsby, Lieutenant Colonel R.D.
  Gardner (w), Major H.J. Williams
4th Virginia
5th Virginia
27th Virginia
33rd Virginia

Taliaferro's Brigade—Colonel James W. Jackson (w), Colonel James L.
  Sheffield
47th Alabama
48th Alabama
23rd Virginia
37th Virginia

Jones's Brigade—Captain John E. Penn (w), Captain A.C. Page (w),
  Captain R.W. Withers
21st Virginia
42nd Virginia
48th Virginia
1st Virginia Battalion

Starke's Brigade—Brigadier General William E. Starke, Colonel Leroy A. Stafford (w), Colonel Edmund Pendleton
1st Louisiana
2nd Louisiana
9th Louisiana
10th Louisiana
15th Louisiana
1st Louisiana Battalion

Artillery—Major L.M. Shumaker
Alleghany Virginia Artillery Carpenter's Battery
Danville Virginia Artillery Wooding's Battery
Lee Virginia Battery Raine's Battery
Rockbridge Virginia Artillery Poague's Battery
Brockenbrough's Maryland Battery

HILL'S DIVISION—MAJOR GENERAL D.H. HILL
Ripley's Brigade—Brigadier General Roswell S. Ripley (w), Colonel George Doles
4th Georgia
44th Georgia
1st North Carolina
3rd North Carolina

Rodes's Brigade—Brigadier General Robert E. Rodes
3rd Alabama
5th Alabama
6th Alabama
12th Alabama
26th Alabama

Garland's Brigade—Colonel D.K. McRae
5th North Carolina
12th North Carolina
13th North Carolina
20th North Carolina
23rd North Carolina

Anderson's Brigade—Brigadier General George B. Anderson (mw),
　Colonel C.C. Tew (k), Colonel R.T. Bennett
2nd North Carolina
4th North Carolina
14th North Carolina
30th North Carolina

Colquitt's Brigade—Brigadier General Alfred H. Colquitt
13th Alabama
6th Georgia
23rd Georgia
27th Georgia
28th Georgia

Artillery—Major C.F. Pierson
Jones's Virginia Battery
King William Virginia Artillery
Hardaway's Alabama Battery
Jeff Davis Alabama Artillery

Appendix 2

Special Orders No. 191

Special Orders, Hdqrs. Army of Northern Virginia
Numbers 191.
September 9, 1862.

I. The citizens of Fredericktown being unwilling, while overrun by members of this army, to pen their stores, in order to give them confidence, and to secure to officers and men purchasing supplies for benefit of this command, all officers and men of this army are strictly prohibited from visiting Fredericktown except on business, in which case they will bear evidence of this in writing from division commanders. The provost-marshal in Fredericktown will see that his guard rigidly enforces this order.

II. Major Taylor will proceed to Leesburg, Va., and arrange for transportation of the sick and those unable to walk to Winchester, securing the transportation of the country for this purpose. The route between this and Culpeper Court-House east of the mountains being unsafe will no longer be traveled. Those on the way to this army already across the river will move up promptly; all others will proceed to Winchester collectively and under command of officers, at which point, being the general depot of this army, its movements will be known and instructions given by commanding officer regulating further movements.

III. The army will resume its march to-morrow, taking the Hagerstown road. General Jackson's command will from the advance, and, after passing Middletown, with such portion as he may select, take the route toward Sharpsburg, cross the Potomac at the most convenient point, and by Friday morning take possession of the Baltimore and Ohio Railroad, capture such of them as may be at Martinsburg, and intercept such as may attempt to escape from Harper's Ferry.

IV. General Longstreet's command will pursue the main road as far as Boonsborough, where it will halt, with reserve, supply, and baggage trains of the army.

V. General McLaws, with his own division and that of General R. H. Anderson, will follow General Longstreet. On reaching Middletown will take the route to Harper's Ferry, and by Friday morning possess himself of the Maryland Heights and endeavor to capture the enemy at harper's Ferry and vicinity.

VI. General Walker, with his division, after accomplishing the object in which he is now engaged, will cross the Potomac at Cheek's Ford, ascend its right bank to Lovettsville, take possession of Loudoun Heights, if practicable, by Friday morning, Keys' Ford on his left, and the road between the end of the mountain and the Potomac on his right. He will, as far as practicable, co-operate with Generals McLaws and Jackson, and intercept retreat of the enemy.

VII. General D.H. Hill's division will form the rear guard of the army, pursing the road taken by the main body. The reserve artillery, ordnance, and supply trains, &c., will precede General Hill.

VIII. General Stuart will detach a squadron of cavalry to accompany the commands of Generals Longstreet, Jackson, and McLaws, and, with the main body of the cavalry, will cover the route of the army, bringing up all stragglers that may have been left behind.

IX. The commands of Generals Jackson, McLaws, and Walker, after accomplishing the objects for which they have been detached, will join the main body of the army at Boonsborough or Hagerstown.

X. Each regiment on the march will habitually carry its axes in the regimental ordnance wagons, for use of the men at their encampments, to procure wood, &c.

By command of General R.E. Lee
R.H. CHILTON,
Assistant Adjutant-General

Note: Articles I and II of this order were not included in the copy received by General McClellan.

Robert E. Lee's Proclamation
to the People of Maryland

To the People of Maryland
Headquarters, Army of Northern Virginia
Near Fredericktown
September 8, 1862

It is right that you should know the purpose that brought the army under my command within the limits of your State, so far as the purpose concerns yourselves.

The people of the Confederate States have long watched with deepest sympathy the wrongs and outrages that have been inflicted upon the citizens of a commonwealth allied to the States of the South by the strongest social, political, and commercial ties.

They have seen profound indignations their sister State deprived of every right and reduced to the conditioned of a conquered province. Under the pretense of supporting the Constitution, but in violation of its most valuable provisions, your citizens have been arrested and imprisoned upon no charge and contrary to all forms of law. The faithful and manly protests against this outrage made by the venerable and illustrious Marylander, to whom in better days no citizen appealed for the right in vain was treated with scorn and contempt; the government of your chief city has been usurped by armed strangers; your legislature has been dissolved by unlawful arrest of its members; freedom of the press and of speech had been suppressed; words have been declared offensive by an arbitrary decree of the Federal

Executive, and citizens ordered to be tried by a military commission for what they may dare to speak.

Believing that the people of Maryland possessed a spirit too lofty to submit to such government, the people of the South have long wished to aid you in throwing off the foreign yoke, to inalienable rights of freemen, and restore independence and sovereignty to your State.

In obedience to this wish, our army has come among you, and is prepared to assist you with the power of its arms in regaining the rights of which you have been despoiled.

This, citizens of Maryland, is our mission, so far as you are concerned.

No constraint upon your free will is intended; no intimidation will be allowed within the limits of this army, at least. Marylanders shall once more enjoy their ancient freedom of thought and speech.

We know no enemies among you, and will protect all, of every opinion.

It is for you to decide your destiny freely and without constraint.

This army will respect your choice, whatever it may be; and while the Southern people will rejoice to welcome you to your natural position among them, they will only welcome you when you come of your own free will.

R.E. LEE,
General Commanding

Notes

Introduction

1. Buell, *Warrior Generals*, 93.
2. See Rowland, *George B. McClellan and Civil War History*.

Chapter 1

3. Donald, *Lincoln*, 329–30; Rafuse, *McClellan's War*, 171.
4. Donald, *Lincoln*, 330.
5. McClellan, *McClellan's Own Story*, 181; Rowland, *George B. McClellan and Civil War History*, 51.
6. Donald, *Lincoln*, 326; Rafuse, *McClellan's War*, 169.
7. Donald, *Lincoln*, 365.
8. Ibid., 365–66.
9. McPherson, *Battle Cry of Freedom*, 423.
10. *The War of the Rebellion: A Compilation of the Official Records of the Union and Confederate Armies* (hereafter referred to as *OR*), ser. 1, vol. 11, pt. 3, 456.
11. Catton, *Mr. Lincoln's Army*, 108.
12. *OR*, ser. 1, vol. 11, 473–74.
13. *OR*, ser. 1, vol. 11, pt. 3, 380.
14. Patrick, *Inside Lincoln's Army*, 140.

Chapter 2

15. McClellan to Ellen Marcy McClellan, September 5, 1862.
16. Rafuse, *McClellan's War*, 49, 59.
17. Ibid., 1.
18. Rapoport, *Clausewitz on War*, 401–3.
19. Catton, *Mr. Lincoln's Army*, 120.
20. Harsh, "On the McClellan-Go-Round," 115–16.
21. Vermilya, *That Field of Blood*, 104.
22. Catton, *Mr. Lincoln's Army*, 103.
23. McPherson, *Battle Cry of Freedom*, 425.
24. Rafuse, *McClellan's War*, 207.
25. McClellan, *McClellan's Own Story*, 186; Catton, *Mr. Lincoln's Army*, 107.
26. McPherson, *Battle Cry of Freedom*, 425.
27. McClellan, *McClellan's Own Story*, 394.
28. *OR*, ser. 1, vol. 11, pt. 3, 456.
29. Ibid., 215.
30. McClellan, *McClellan's Own Story*, 303–4; McPherson, *Battle Cry of Freedom*, 460; Rowland, *George B. McClellan and Civil War History*, 212.
31. Rowland, *George B. McClellan and Civil War History*, 112.
32. Ibid., 275.
33. *OR*, ser. 1, vol. 11, pt. 1, 46.
34. Rowland, *George B. McClellan and Civil War History*, 119.
35. Rafuse, *McClellan's War*, 232.
36. McClellan, *McClellan's Own Story*, 536.
37. Ibid., 73–74.
38. Ibid., 245.
39. Donald, *Lincoln*, 369–70.
40. Ibid., 235.
41. Ibid., 61.
42. Catton, *Mr. Lincoln's Army*, 142.
43. Rafuse, *McClellan's War*, 253.
44. McClellan, *McClellan's Own Story*, 609.
45. Rafuse, *McClellan's War*, 257.
46. McPherson, *Battle Cry of Freedom*, 529.
47. *OR*, ser. 1, vol. 12, 739–41.
48. Catton, *Mr. Lincoln's Army*, 1.
49. Donald, *Lincoln*, 361.
50. Ibid., 155.

51. Rafuse, *McClellan's War*, 148; Frye, *Antietam Shadows*, 202.

Chapter 3

52. See Thomas, *Robert E. Lee*, chapter 20.
53. Rapoport, *Clausewitz on War*, 342.
54. Ibid., 128–29.
55. McPherson, *Battle Cry of Freedom*, 461, 465–70.
56. *OR*, ser. 1, vol. 19, pt. 2, 604–5.
57. Donald, *Lincoln*, 313, 454.
58. *OR*, ser. 1, vol. 19, pt. 2, 592.

Chapter 4

59. Donald, *Lincoln*, 373–74.

Chapter 5

60. McPherson, *Battle Cry of Freedom*, 115.
61. *OR*, ser. 1, vol. 19, pt. 2, 605–6.
62. Longstreet, *From Manassas to Appomattox*, 173–74.
63. *OR*, ser. 1, vol. 19, pt. 2, 169.
64. Longstreet, *From Manassas to Appomattox*, 179; Rafuse, *McClellan's War*, 279.
65. Frye, *Antietam Shadows*, 124.
66. Ibid., 122.
67. Rafuse, *McClellan's War*, 291.
68. *OR*, ser. 1, vol. 19, pt. 1, 118.
69. Ibid., 30.
70. Fishel, *Untold Story of Military Intelligence*, 102–4; Rafuse, *McClellan's War*, 131.
71. Gibbon, *At Gettysburg and Elsewhere*, 58.
72. *OR*, ser. 1, vol. 19, pt. 2, 281.
73. Ibid., 254–55.
74. *Numbers and Losses at Battle of Antietam*; Vermilya, *That Field of Blood*, 73.
75. Catton, *Mr. Lincoln's Army*, 222.

76. *OR*, ser. 1, vol. 19, pt. 1, 146.
77. McClellan, *McClellan's Own Story*, 632.

Chapter 6

78. *OR*, ser. 1, vol. 19, pt. 1, 1,022; Vermilya, *That Field of Blood*, 104.
79. *OR*, ser. 1, vol. 19, pt. 1, 1,022.
80. McClellan, *McClellan's Own Story*, 45.
81. *OR*, ser. 1, vol. 19, pt. 2, 289.
82. *OR*, ser. 1, vol. 50, pt. 2, 618–19.
83. Ibid., 606.
84. *OR*, ser. 1, vol. 19, pt. 1, 891.
85. *OR*, ser. 1, vol. 19, pt. 2, 296–97.
86. Ibid., 294–95.
87. *OR*, ser. 1, vol. 19, pt. 1, 121.
88. *Numbers and Losses at Battle of Antietam*; Vermilya, *That Field of Blood*, 28.
89. Vermilya, *That Field of Blood*, 47.
90. *Numbers and Losses at Battle of Antietam*.
91. McClellan, *McClellan's Own Story*, 650.
92. *OR*, ser. 1, vol. 19, pt. 1, 30.
93. Frye, *Antietam Shadows*, 146, 162.
94. Sears, *Landscape Turned Red*, 310.
95. *OR*, ser. 1, vol. 11, pt. 1, 47.

Chapter 7

96. Ibid., 189–200.
97. Ibid., 810–14.
98. Sears, *Landscape Turned Red*, 309.
99. Rodenbough et al., *Photographic History of the Civil War*, 158.
100. McClellan, *McClellan's Own Story*, 650.
101. *OR*, ser. 1, vol. 19, pt. 1, 218.
102. Ibid., 56.
103. Ibid., 129.
104. Ibid., 56; Rafuse, *McClellan's War*, 315–18.
105. *OR*, ser. 1, vol. 19, pt. 1, 56.
106. *OR*, ser. 1, vol. 19, pt. 2, 297.

107. Frye, *Antietam Shadows*, 170.
108. *OR*, ser. 1, vol. 19, pt. 1, 981.
109. Ibid., 377.
110. Longstreet, *From Manassas to Appomattox*, 230.
111. Ibid.
112. Rafuse, *McClellan's War*, 327–28; Vermilya, *That Field of Blood*, 800.
113. Rafuse, *McClellan's War*, 332.
114. Vermilya, *That Field of Blood*, 117.
115. *OR*, ser. 1, vol. 19, pt. 2, 330.

Chapter 8

116. McClellan to Ellen Marcy McClellan, September 29, 1862.
117. *Weekly Standard Journal*, September 22, 1862. The editorial referenced the *Richmond Enquirer* quote re: Sharpsburg as "[o]ne of the most complete victories."
118. *Numbers and Losses at Battle of Antietam*.
119. Longstreet, *From Manassas to Appomattox*, 229.
120. McClellan, *McClellan's Own Story*, 668; *OR*, ser. 1, vol. 19, pt. 1, 181.
121. *OR*, ser. 1, vol. 19, pt. 1, 7–24.
122. Ibid., 13–14.
123. Rafuse, *McClellan's War*, 349.
124. Ibid., 351.

Chapter 9

125. Rowland, *George B. McClellan and Civil War History*, 74–75.
126. Ibid., 231.
127. Donald, *Lincoln*, 385–86.
128. Ibid., 34, 140, 173; Murfin, *Gleam of Bayonets*; Palfrey, *Antietam and Fredericksburg*.
129. Supporters of General McClellan dispute that destroying the enemy was ever considered by him—while using phrasing such as "destroy" Lee's subordinates (footnote 20), "severely punish" (footnote 16), "whip" (footnote 15), instructions to Franklin to "Destroy" McLaws's command (*OR*, ser. 1, vol. 19, pt. 1, 47) and in communications with Governor Curtin of Pennsylvania to "destroy any army" (*OR*, ser. 1, vol. 19, pt. 1, 249).

130. Rafuse, *McClellan's War*, 157.

131. Ibid., 126.

132. Donald, *Lincoln*, 338–39.

133. *OR*, ser. 1, vol. 19, pt. 2, 184–85.

134. Frye, *Antietam Shadows*, 126.

135. Rafuse, *McClellan's War*, 113.

136. Ibid., 240.

137. *OR*, ser. 1, vol. 19, pt. 1, 179.

138. Ibid., 209.

139. Rafuse, *McClellan's War*, 288.

140. Sears, *Landscape Turned Red*, 120.

141. Rafuse, *McClellan's War*, 294.

142. Gottfried, *Maps of Antietam…Including the Battle of South Mountain*, 46–89.

143. McClellan, *McClellan's Own Story*, 682, 686; *OR*, ser. 1, vol. 19, pt. 1, 66.

144. McClellan, *McClellan's Own Story*, 688.

145. *OR*, ser. 1, vol. 19, pt. 2, 353.

146. *OR*, ser. 1, vol. 19, pt. 1, 7–24.

147. Rafuse, *McClellan's War*, 335; Rowland, *George B. McClellan and Civil War History*, 88, 199.

148. Rowland, *George B. McClellan and Civil War History*, 109.

149. Moore, *Rebellion Record*, 5:465.

150. Sears, *Landscape Turned Red*, 325; Donald, *Lincoln*, 387; Rafuse, *McClellan's War*, 344.

151. *OR*, ser. 1, vol. 19, pt. 2, 16–17.

152. Ibid., 484–85; McClellan, *McClellan's Own Story*, 698.

153. *OR*, ser. 3, vol. 2, 703–4.

154. Ibid., 10–11.

155. *OR*, ser. 1, vol. 19, pt. 1, 13–14.

156. Randall, *Lincoln the President*, 2:323.

157. Ibid., 233.

158. Buell, *Warrior Generals*, 448.

159. Longstreet, *From Manassas to Appomattox*, 174–75.

160. Rowland, *George B. McClellan and Civil War History*, 225.

161. Frye, *Antietam Shadows*, 187.

162. *OR*, ser. 1, vol. 24, pt. 3, 157.

163. Rafuse, *McClellan's War*, 383–85.

Bibliography

Books

Buell, Thomas B. *The Warrior Generals: Combat Leadership in the Civil War.* New York: Three Rivers Press, 1997.

Catton, Bruce. *Mr. Lincoln's Army.* New York: Doubleday and Company, 1951.
———. *The Picture History of the Civil War.* N.p.: American Heritage, 1960.

Donald, David Herbert. *Lincoln.* New York: Simon and Schuster, 1995.

Fishel, Edwin C. *The Untold Story of Military Intelligence in the Civil War.* Boston: Houghton Mifflin, 1996.

Foote, Shelby. *Civil War: A Narrative.* New York: Random House, 1963.

Frassanito, William A. *Antietam: The Photographic Legacy of America's Bloodiest Day.* N.p.: Thomas Publications, 1978.

Frye, Dennis E. *Antietam Shadows: Mystery, Myth & Machinations.* N.p.: Antietam Rest Publications, 2018.

Gibbon, John. *At Gettysburg and Elsewhere: Personal Recollections.* N.p.: Big Byte Books, 2016.

Gottfried, Bradley M. *The Maps of Antietam: An Atlas of the Antietam (Sharpsburg) Campaign, Including the Battle of South Mountain.* El Dorado Hills, CA: Savas Beatie, 2012.
———. *The Maps of Antietam: An Atlas of the Antietam (Sharpsburg) Campaign, the Siege and Capture of Harper's Ferry.* El Dorado Hills, CA: Savas Beatie, 2012.

Lee, Captain Robert E. *Recollections and Letters of General Robert E. Lee.* N.p.: Konecky & Konecky.

Longstreet, James. *From Manassas to Appomattox: Memoirs of the Civil War in America*. 1896. Reprint, Lyndhurst, NJ: Barnes & Noble Publishing, 2004.

McClellan, George B. *McClellan's Own Story*. New York, 1887. Reprint, Big Byte Books, 2014.

McPherson, James M. *Battle Cry of Freedom: The Civil War Era*. New York: Ballantine Books, 1989.

———. *Crossroads of Freedom: Antietam*. New York: Oxford Press, 2002.

Moore, Frank, ed. *The Rebellion Record*. 5th vol. N.p.: G.P. Putnam, 1868.

Murfin, James V. *The Gleam of Bayonets: The Battle of Antietam and the Maryland Campaign*. N.p.: A.S. Barnes & Company, 1964.

Palfrey, Francis Winthrop. *The Antietam and Fredericksburg*. New York: Charles Scribner's Sons, 1882.

Patrick, Marsena. *Inside Lincoln's Army: The Diary of Marcena Rudolph Patrick, Provost Marshall General*. N.p.: T. Yoseloff, 1964.

Rafuse, Ethen S. *McClellan's War*. Bloomington: Indiana University Press, 2005.

Randall, J.G. *Lincoln the President: Springfield to Gettysburg*, Vol. 2. New York: Dodd, Mead & Company, 1945.

Rapoport, Anatol, ed. *Clausewitz on War*. Berlin: Vom Kriege Publishing, 1832. Reprint, Penguin Books, 1968.

Rhodes, James Ford. *A History of the Civil War, 1861–1865*. New York: Macmillan Publishers, 1917.

Rodenbough, Theo, F. Lainier, Robert S. Elson and Henry W. Elson, eds. *The Photographic History of the Civil War, Armies & Leaders*. N.p.: Fairfax Press, 1983, 1989 edition.

Rowland, Thomas J. *George B. McClellan and Civil War History*. Kent, OH: Kent State University Press, 1998.

Sears, Stephen W. *Landscape Turned Red*. New York: Houghton Mifflin Company, 1983.

———. *Lincoln's Lieutenants: The High Command of the Army of the Potomac*. Boston: Houghton Mifflin Harcourt, 2017.

Stahl, Joseph, and Matthew Borders. *Faces of Union Soldiers at Antietam*. Charleston, SC: The History Press, 2019.

Stotelmyer, Steven R. *Too Useful to Sacrifice*. El Dorado Hills, CA: Savas Beatie, 2019.

Thomas, Emory M. *Robert E. Lee*. New York: W.W. Norton & Company, 1997.

Vermilya, Daniel J. *That Field of Blood: The Battle of Antietam*. El Dorado Hills, CA: Savas Beatie, 2018.

Warner, Ezra J. *Generals in Blue*. Baton Rouge: Louisiana State University Press, 1964.

———. *Generals in Gray*. Baton Rouge: Louisiana State University Press, 1959.

Wheeler, Tom. *Mr. Lincoln's T-Mail*. New York: HarperCollins, 2008.

Newspaper

Weekly Standard Journal (Raleigh, NC). September 22, 1862.

Other

Harsh, Joseph L. "On the McClellan-Go-Round." *Civil War History* (June 1973).

Interview of Joseph L. Harsh by William J. Miller, March 10, 2015.

McClellan to Ellen Marcy McClellan. McClellan Papers, Library of Congress.

Numbers and Losses at Battle of Antietam. NPS Handout, ANB. Undated.

The War of the Rebellion: A Compilation of the Official Records of the Union and Confederate Armies. Available at Cornell University Library.

Index

ABOUT THE AUTHOR

D AVID KELLER is a longtime resident of Chicago and an amateur historian. Mr. Keller was a distinguished military graduate serving in command positions in Germany and served on the staff of General William Westmorland in Vietnam. Retired from the business community since 2002, he devotes much of his time to volunteer activities, including at the Chicago History Museum. He is founder and managing director of the Camp Douglas Restoration Foundation and editor of its newsletter, *Camp Douglas News*. Mr. Keller's previous books are *Military Prisons of the American Civil War: A Comparative Study*, *The Story of Camp Douglas: Chicago's Forgotten Civil War Prison* and *Robert Anderson Bagby: Civil War Diary (Annotated) 1863–1865*. He has published two studies on Civil War prison camps for the National Park Service, Andersonville National Site POW Research Program. He has also provided a number of articles for periodicals. David and his wife, Linda, split their time between Chicago and a home in the Indiana Dunes National Park, where David continues to write on Civil War topics.